D1485805

EXPLORING ENGLAND

EXPLORING ENGLAND

AN INTRODUCTION TO NATURE CRAFT

by

CHARLES S. BAYNE

"SQUIRREL"

With Illustrations by C. F. TUNNICLIFFE

COLLINS

LONDON AND GLASGOW

Dragonfly

PRINTED AND MADE IN GREAT BRITAIN
BY WM. COLLINS SONS AND CO. LTD.
LONDON AND GLASGOW

CONTENTS

ILLUSTRATIONS

In Line

CHAPTER ONE

FIELDS

To taste the full joy of exploration it is not necessary to go to the ends of the earth. Such adventures are reserved for the giants among us. There is a vast world of interest at our very doors which, to be understood and enjoyed, must be discovered anew by each one of us individually, and in which indeed there is still plenty of scope for original research. In the following chapters I am going to give a few hints as to the secrets that may be revealed there to a keen hunter, and it is my earnest hope that I may thereby send many a good nature lover forth on the great adventure of exploring his own country.

Unfortunately there are very few mammals still living wild in England. The rabbit is the only one you may be sure to find in its natural haunts any day in the week. You may fairly frequently see the hare, the squirrel and the

9

water vole and sometimes by chance a stoat or a weasel, but all the others are so shy or so nocturnal in their habits that you will be lucky if you ever catch a glimpse of them.

On the other hand a good observer may see from thirty to fifty different species of bird in the course of an afternoon's walk, and hundreds of species of plant. Wherever there are plants there are also insects and birds, and there may be mammals too, though they may have to be searched for, besides many other lower forms of life.

Now, in any ordinary walk you are sure to pass through more than one type of land. There will be fields and woods of various kinds, probably ditches and streams, ponds or lakes, farms and villages, and there may be dry heaths or marshy wastes, or you may be in hilly, moorland or mountainous districts, or by the sea coast which may be sandy or rocky, flat or cliffbound. Each kind of locality has its own charm as scenery, but it also has its own wealth of plant and animal life, which to the seeing eye and listening ear adds infinitely to its interest. It must be remembered, however, that animals, being mobile creatures, are given to wandering, and moreover, they are endowed with a considerable amount of enterprise. So it is not possible to lay down hard and fast rules about their habits. Some of them may be found in various kinds of country, and others may astonish you at any moment by appearing in most unexpected places. Such surprises are not only extremely interesting in themselves, but they also make the rules, such as they are, doubly interesting.

For example, in the open fields you cannot go far without coming upon the rabbit. We may say that it is one of the regular inhabitants of our fields, but it is also common wherever there is herbage on which it can feed, from the seaside to the mountain tops.

Rabbits live in colonies, making homes for themselves by digging deep burrows in the ground. These burrows have more than one entrance. The main door is usually quite open, but the others are often hidden among long grass or bracken. So if an enemy makes his way in at the front door the rabbits pop out at the back.

These burrows are more or less common property, so they are not suitable places for a nursery. They are really only public living-rooms. It is not the custom for a pair of rabbits to make a burrow for themselves and to rear their families in it. Indeed, when a litter is born the old buck is a useless and dangerous member of the household. So when a doe expects a family she prepares a special burrow at a little distance from the general warren. This is a short tunnel with a wide chamber at the end and no back exit. In it the doe builds a nest with grass which she tears up in great bundles and carries there in her mouth, and she lines it with down from her own breast. When the family is born she leaves them alone during the day, but before she goes she is careful to fill up the entrance to the burrow with earth, so that no prowling hunters may find them. She returns to feed them in the evening and in the early morning, removing and replacing the earth each time.

Though you may see rabbits abroad at any time of the day, it is their custom to rest while the sun is up and to come out in the evening to feed. They sleep either in the burrow or well hidden among long grass at some distance from it. Even at feeding time, however, they never go very far from home, but the colony may scatter itself half across the field. Then if anything should happen to alarm them they signal to each other in a peculiar way.

As a rule they are very silent creatures. They are able to grunt, and no doubt at close quarters they can express something in this manner. But their alarm signal is given by striking the ground forcibly with their strong hind feet. This makes a resounding thump like the fall of a heavy stone. If you can post yourself at some point of vantage and wait patiently and keep perfectly still, you may both hear this remarkable warning and see it being done, and then watch the result.

Now, any one at first sight can see that the hare is related to the rabbit. It has the same general form (though its legs are longer in proportion to its size), and similar ears. It is also an inhabitant of the fields, but it is a solitary creature and very shy. If you make a practice of looking over gates and stiles you may see it quite frequently, but usually alone. It is seldom that you will find more than two together. Size is always an uncertain guide to a beginner, but you may readily know a hare by its ears, for their tips are black.

When a rabbit is alarmed it sits up on its haunches and pricks up its ears to gain further information. Then, if it fears danger, it bolts for its burrow with its ears lying flat on its neck. For a few yards it goes at a great pace, but it could not keep this up for long distances. On the other hand the hare has no burrow and depends for its safety entirely on its speed and cunning. When it is startled a hare makes off at an easy canter, keeping its ears erect to ascertain whether it is being followed. Only when some foe is in hot pursuit does it lay its ears back and stretch out to its full speed. What a wonderful sight it is then! It seems to be skimming the ground, yet at each bound it covers ten feet or more. It is not a high jumper, however, so you are never likely to see it spring over a fence. It invariably enters and leaves a field by the gate or by some break in the wall or hedge.

When a hare is resting it lies hidden in what is called a

form, that is a tunnel which it shapes with its body in a tuft of long grass, the tops of which make a roof. Often when you are crossing a meadow a hare may spring from its form almost at your feet. You will then see what a snug hiding-place it can make where you might think that such a large animal could find no cover.

The young are born in such a form. There are usually two or three in a litter, but you may consider yourself lucky if you ever find a family at home. If you do they will be almost new born, for they come into the world fully clothed with fur and with their eyes wide open, and a day or two later they separate, each making a form of its own. Thus if one of them is discovered by a fox or any enemy of the race, the others may escape. Rabbits on the other hand, which are reared in a cosy nest in a burrow, are born naked and blind.

Other common mammal residents of the fields are the hedgehog, the mole and the field mice. The hedgehog and the mole belong to a different family from the rabbit and the hare. They are insect eaters. The hedgehog is seldom seen during the day. As a rule, he lies hidden then in a snug bed of old leaves in some hedge-bottom or other suitable place. But if you visit the fields after dusk you are almost certain to see him. He comes out under cover of the darkness to feed on beetles, grubs, slugs and so on. You may even hear him before you see him, for while he plods along in his old-man fashion, he grunts with satisfaction as he goes.

The moment he hears you approaching he will tuck in his head and his tail and curl himself into a ball. You will then see how wonderfully he is protected. The curling causes his spines to bristle in all directions, so that no tender-nosed marauder may touch him without suffering for his daring.

The mole works all day, but he is able to do so only

because he lives in a tunnel. Except in very dry weather when the earth is baked hard by the sun, he seldom comes out on the surface. But you may often see the effects of his work. As he mines his way in search of worms and grubs the ground heaves as if in a small earthquake, and if you stop in time and watch patiently, you may be lucky enough to spy his little pink nose push its way through among the grass. Or you may witness the rise of a molehill, which grows like a small volcano. The mole drags to the shaft all the loose earth it has excavated to form its tunnels, and thrusts it upward with its nose so that it pours out at the top of the cone and tumbles down the sides.

The nest is not placed inside a molehill, but is built underneath a specially large one and several inches underground. There may be many molehills in the territory of a single mole, for when the little miner pushes its workings rather far from the original shaft, it opens a new shaft and starts a second hill. When you see several molehills more or less in a straight line you may be sure they represent the workings of a male and you need not look for a nest among them. The workings of a female are indicated by a number of hills in an irregular group.

The shrew is mouselike in form and colour, but it is really another insect-eater. You may know it by its long tapir-like snout which it uses to grub in the earth for worms and larvæ.

There are two kinds of field mouse, the long-tailed and the short-tailed. The former is similar to the common mouse, but instead of being grey it is reddish-brown above and white underneath. The short-tailed field mouse, or grass mouse, or field vole as it is variously called, is only a distant cousin of the mice. It is a charming little round-nosed furry creature with a hairy tail. Both species are nocturnal in habit, but they do feed at intervals during the day. At such times you may be fortunate enough to see them, and the hints I have given will enable you to identify them.

Now, the presence of mice in a field attracts there two other very different creatures, namely, the kestrel and the owl, both of which are birds of prey.

At least once in the course of a day's tramp you are sure to see a large brown bird with a long round-tipped tail, hovering high up in the air above a field. Most people will tell you it is a hawk. It is a member of the hawk tribe, but it belongs to the falcon branch of the family, and its proper name is kestrel. If you watch it you will find that it is a perfect weathercock, for whenever it wishes to hover it turns its head to the wind. The reason for this is obvious, for as the wind travels in one direction at a certain speed, a bird that flies against it at the same pace will remain stationary. If you get a close view of it, you will see that it uses its tail for balancing by spreading it and as a brake by depressing it.

The kestrel's object in hovering is to look for its prey, which consists chiefly of mice and beetles, and when its keen eyes discover a tell-tale movement on the ground, it descends and captures the unwary venturer, grasping it in its talons. But you may observe it travelling far and hovering many times before it succeeds.

After dusk, and even sometimes in broad daylight, you may see another hunter of mice at work in the fields. Its methods are quite different from those of the kestrel. Instead of hovering, it floats along on silent wings close to the ground, and passes first up the field then down, then up again with the regularity of a farmer sowing seed. The mice are then much more active, but nevertheless you may watch an owl thus quartering a whole field without once making a capture.

There are several species of owl, but those you are most likely to see are the barn owl and the brown owl. The barn owl is white, except for its back which is light chestnut, but this colour is of course not noticeable in the darkness. If you hear the bird call you may know it to be the brown owl if it shouts *kee-wick* or *to-whoo*. The note of the barn owl is a startling eldritch screech.

There are many other bird visitors to the fields. Rooks, jackdaws, starlings and black-headed gulls go there in flocks. They feed on much smaller fare than is required by kestrel and owl, so they are kept constantly busy picking up little tit-bits. These consist chiefly of the larvæ and pupæ of insects which at those stages of their development hide in the earth, especially those of the daddy-longlegs (leather jacket) of the click-beetle (wireworm) and of the Maybug or cockchafer, which do enormous damage to crops by eating the roots of growing plants.

The blackbird, the song-thrush and the missel-thrush feed largely upon worms which they find in the fields. You should note that the hen blackbird is not black but brown, and that the missel-thrush is most easily distinguished from the song-thrush by its larger size, by a white feather on each side of its tail, by its dipping flight, and by its harsh rattling call.

In autumn and winter two other members of the thrush tribe visit our fields, namely, the redwing and the fieldfare. The redwing is about the size of the song-thrush, but has a conspicuous buff stripe above the eye and the red on its flanks and underwing is very noticeable when it raises its wings. The fieldfare is almost as large as the missel-thrush, and may always be recognised by its light grey neck and rump and its chestnut back. Both these birds are foreigners, and come regularly from the far north to spend the winter

Rooks, jackdaws, starlings and black-headed gulls go there in flocks.

in our more genial climate. They keep together in flocks.

Pigeons also visit the fields for food, often in large flocks. The commonest are the wood pigeon and the stock dove. When you know them well you can identify them by their flight, but the simplest distinction between them is that the wood pigeon has a large white patch on each wing which is very conspicuous when the bird is flying.

Again, in winter you will often see large flocks of small birds feeding in ploughed fields and stubble. They are picking up the seeds of the many weeds that flourished among the crops in summer. Some flocks may consist entirely of chaffinches, in which case they may be either all cocks or all hens, a peculiarity from which the bird has been named the bachelor. Other flocks may be all gold-finches. When you meet with them, put them to flight and watch the exquisite flash of gold from their wings as they turn together in the sunlight. Many flocks, however, will include both sexes of chaffinch, goldfinch, greenfinch, and other members of the finch family.

All these birds are visitors to the fields. A number of species spend the whole, or the greater part of their lives there. The partridge is peculiarly a bird of the open fields. You may often see it from the road, calmly stepping about and picking up seeds, or when crossing a turnip field or a meadow you may be startled by a pair or a whole family of partridges rising from under your feet and, with a great whirring of wings, flying heavily over the hedge.

There are two species of partridge, the common and the red-legged. You are not likely to see the legs of the latter, but you may easily identify the bird by the fact that it has a white gorget, a black collar, a black stripe through the eye and a white stripe above it, and a number of black and white vertical markings on its side.

Each pair of partridges keeps to itself and rears a large family. Old and young remain together all winter, the family as a whole being known as a covey. Then, if they have not been shot by sportsmen, the parents drive off the young one by one to seek homes and mates of their own.

Lapwings on the other hand always live in flocks. In spring they migrate to the upland fields and there they settle down in open formation, each pair owning its own section of a field and attending to its own affairs, yet keeping close enough in touch with its neighbours to join them in a demonstration against some passing crow or other possible enemy. It is a thrilling experience to listen to them calling, *tcher-willooch-weet*, as they plunge and tumble in the first rapture of spring over their nesting field.

When the nesting season is over, the flock draws together again and migrates to the lowlands and the coast, where it spends the winter in damp meadows and marshes.

Another field bird with a remarkable call is the corn-crake. This bird is rare in the south of England where it used to be common. It seems to have been driven out by the reaping machine. But farther north and in Scotland, where the harvest is later, it is still common. Even there, however, though you cannot help hearing its harsh craking note, you will very seldom see it unless you are a skilled and very patient observer. For, whereas it flies from and to Africa every spring and autumn, it spends most of its time in this country skulking among hay and growing corn. It used to have the reputation of being a ventriloquist, because as you listen to its call, the sound seems one moment to come from close at hand, and the next from the other side of the field. But if you are ever skilful or lucky enough to see it while it is craking you will notice that it turns its head now this way now that, and this causes the changes in the sound. Its object, of course, is to attract its mate in whatever part of the field she may be.

The great song of the fields, however, is the skylark's, and it is all the more interesting because of the manner in which it is delivered. The common belief is that the skylark sings while it is soaring up to the sky. That is true, but if you take the trouble to watch the bird throughout the spring and summer you will notice that it varies its method at different seasons. I have seen a skylark singing while it was hovering only six feet from the ground, another while it was sitting on the top of a haystack, and yet another while it was standing on a stone by the roadside. Such variations occur either early or late in the season. In February or March while pairing is in progress, the bird will mount fifty or a hundred feet into the air and sing while it is fluttering round in wide circles; or it will soar still higher and, shortly after it begins to descend, it will close its wings and drop silently like a stone to the ground. But in the height of the nesting season, on calm, sunny days in May and June I have lain on my back in a field and watched skylarks sing from the moment they have sprung from the ground till they have vanished into the blue sky, and from the time they have reappeared descending till their feet have almost touched the grass.

In fields where there are trees you may see a more beautiful performance by the tree pipit, which is a cousin of the skylark and visits us only in summer. This little bird has a much shorter song than the skylark's, but one with a more definite form, and he often repeats it when he is sitting on a twig, bubbling over with excitement the while. But suddenly he will mount obliquely from the tree and, when he is twenty or thirty feet above it, will spread his wings and tail and plane down, singing throughout the descent till he reaches his perch again. You can never mistake the bird when you see him do this, and you will note that his song always ends with a phrase that sounds like *see-ah*, *see-ah*, *see-ah*.

Now, those leather jackets, wireworms and Maybug grubs that escape the beaks of hungry birds, pass into the chrysalis stage of their development and after lying torpid for some time, emerge into the upper world as fully-equipped flying machines known as cranefly or daddy-longlegs, click-beetle or skipjack, and cockchafer. They then proceed to lay their eggs in the ground, and the mischief begins all over again.

You may easily watch the cranefly doing this, and at the same time you will discover the utility of her absurdly long legs. The female is distinguished from the male by the fact that her tail is sharply pointed. When she is in flight her legs look grotesque, but when she is among the grass they enable her to pass easily and quickly from stalk to stalk. And further, they act as levers by which she can lower herself among the grass stems and deposit her eggs in the ground without having to crawl down and up again each time.

But not all insects are injurious. Grasshoppers are harmless, and butterflies and bees are beneficial. The grasshopper eats grass, biting off a piece from the end of a blade and holding this between his forelegs while he eats it. This operation is very remarkable and is worth observing. So is his musical performance, which is a kind of banjo playing. On the inside of his hind legs he has a little file, and on the outside of his wing a raised rib, which takes the place of the banjo string. It is by drawing the file across the rib that he causes the cheerful whirring sound that we hear so constantly in the meadows on sunny summer days.

The most conspicuous of the field insects, however, are the butterflies by day and the moths by night. There are many species of both, each of which has its own short season. The commonest of the butterflies is the meadow-brown, a large dusky-brown insect with, on each forewing, an orange eye-spot in which there is a black iris and a tiny white pupil. Another very common one is the beautiful little common blue. It is the male that is blue; the female is brown with orange spots on the margin of her wings. Both these butterflies may be seen on the wing almost all summer. The orange tip, a medium sized butterfly with a bright orange patch on the tip of each forewing, has only a short season of a few weeks in May and June. The large, the small, and the green-veined white butterflies have two broods in the year so you may see them from April to June, and again in August and September.

After dusk in June and July you may often see a curious white object dancing in the air two or three feet from the ground, but remaining in one spot as if it were dangling from a thread. This is the male ghost moth. He is not just amusing himself; he is trying to attract a mate. The female is brown and so is hardly visible, and she does not dangle; but if you watch a male you are sure to see a female come to him before long.

These and other species of butterfly and moth are a delight to look upon because of their beautiful colours and their wonderful grace of form and movement. But both they and the bees are most interesting when they visit the flowers.

Buttercups and daisies are the most familiar flowers, but they are so well known that they are generally overlooked. Most people are surprised when they are told that there are at least three common species of buttercup, and that they may all be found growing together in one meadow. They all seem so much alike that we do not notice their differences until we examine them. But look behind the petals of a few plants and you will find that on some the sepals, that is, the little green leaflets which form the bracket in which the petals are placed, are bent backwards till they are touching the stalk. Whenever you see this you may know that you have a bulbous buttercup, so called from the nature of its root. This species is usually not more than a foot in height. In the other species the sepals are spreading. The common buttercup may develop into a tall much-branched plant three feet high or more, and the creeping buttercup sends out long runners among the grass.

The name daisy means simply day's eye, and the flower is supposed to open at sunrise and close at sunset. My experience is that it closes about an hour before the sun goes down. The scarlet pimpernel, which is another common flower of the fields, is known as the farmer's weather glass because it closes more readily than other flowers when the sun is obscured by clouds. It goes to sleep for the day about three o'clock. The goat's beard is tired out and shuts up its petals before midday, and from this it is often called John-go-to-bed-at-noon.

On the other hand the white campion sleeps by day and wakes up at night. The reason for this is that it prefers moths to any other insect visitor, and, as they are night-flying creatures, it offers its honey in the evening and draws attention to its stores by means of its white petals, which, as you may see for yourself, are visible in the darkness.

Now, a plant tempts insects with honey because they fertilise its flowers while they are sipping it. For this purpose bees are more satisfactory than butterflies and moths because their visits are more regular, and many

plants seem to prefer the bumblebee. Such a plant is the
yellow toadflax which grows in the fields and is a wild
cousin of the snapdragon or antirrhinum of our gardens.
The tube of the yellow flower is always closed, but you will
notice that the lips are coloured a rich orange. The bee
notices that also and alights there. Now press the lower lip
with your finger and the mouth will open. That is what
happens when the bee alights; its weight causes the lower
jaw to drop. Inside the mouth you will see two rows of
orange hairs and between them a clear path leading straight
to the honey chamber. The bee does not fail to see that too.

Again, examine a head of common white clover. You
will find that it is just a bunch of tiny pea flowers. Each of
these, after it has been visited by a bee, will develop into a
pod containing seed. But that will take time, and meanwhile something else more remarkable happens. The first
of the flowers to open are those in the lowest row. When
these have been fertilised they droop and wither, and when
the bee calls next day they are hanging down round the
stalk out of her way, and those of the second row are ready
to receive her. And so it goes on till the whole head is
fertilised.

CHAPTER TWO

THE HEDGEROWS

THERE are four-footed furry creatures in the hedgerows and banks of our country lanes, but they are so shy that we very seldom see them. Sometimes you may catch a glimpse of one of them as it crosses the road in front of you, and then if you can stop on the instant and remain perfectly still, you may perhaps have the privilege of watching it hunting or eating or even tending its young. But as a rule these venturesome individuals are so anxious to reach the cover on the other side of the road, that they vanish almost before you have time to identify them. In this way I have learnt some of the secrets of stoat, weasel, squirrel, rat and hedge-hog. The squirrel, of course, does not live in the hedgerow, but crosses the road simply to reach the trees on the other side. Stoat, weasel and rat have their homes in the banks or old walls, and the hedgehog sleeps all day among the dead leaves at the bottom of the hedge, but all of them go abroad to make their living.

There are some dwellers in the hedgerows, however, which spend practically the whole of their lives among the herbage or branches in which their homes are hidden, and seldom, if ever, are bold enough to cross the road except after dusk. These are the shrew, the bank vole and the dormouse. It is quite common, when walking along a lane, to hear a confusion of shrill squeaking coming from among the herbs on the hedge bank. When this happens you may know that a couple of shrews have met and, in accordance with their nature, are indulging in a violent quarrel. If you are quick enough you may even see the little grey forms hurrying away into hiding.

The whole bank is honeycombed with tiny runs which are partly underground and partly on the surface, but more or less roofed in with herbage. Both shrews and bank voles seem to use these indiscriminately, and apparently in quite a friendly way.

The bank vole prefers old hedgerows in which there is much ivy, especially those bordering woods. If you suspect his presence you may tempt him out by making a little pile of nuts or large seeds near his burrow, and you may then have the pleasure of seeing him eat. He sits up on his haunches, squirrel fashion, and holds the food in his forepaws.

He is a good climber, and if you make a practice of examining old nests when the hedges are bare, you may quite often come upon one that has been used as a dining-room by a vole. It will be full of empty nut shells, each with a round hole near the tip, so small that you will wonder how ever the kernel was got through it. The wood mouse also does this, but you may know his dining-room by the fact that the nut shells have a large, ragged hole in their sides.

The dormouse also likes ivy-grown hedges, but prefers those in which there is a profusion of twigs near the ground. He does not burrow but builds a round nest about the size of a cricket ball, which he hides in the thickest part of the hedge and very commonly among the ivy. He is very sleepy all day and if, when you find his nest, you do not disturb him violently, he will probably go to sleep again at once, though, if you really rouse and alarm him, he will disappear as if by magic.

If you return to the same spot in the evening about dusk, you may have the pleasure of watching him at work. Then he is a very different creature. He is as active as a squirrel, and very squirrel-like in his actions, except that he does not curl his tail over his back. When he sits up on a twig to eat a nut or a berry he makes a very charming picture. He also has his own way of eating a nut. Unlike the vole and the mouse, he invariably gnaws a round hole at the broad end, always beginning actually on the light patch. So if you find in the neighbourhood of hazel bushes empty nutshells that have been burgled in this way, you may be sure that a dormouse is not far off.

The birds of the hedgerows do not require to be looked for. They show themselves boldly, attract attention by their plumage and restlessness, and announce their presence by their calls and songs. The most familiar because he is the commonest, the boldest, and the most brilliantly plumed, is the chaffinch. His rosy-breast, blue head, and black wings barred with white, make his identification easy. His mate has similar wings, but the rest of her plumage is a subdued green. By seeing her, however, in company with her lively and conspicuous mate you will soon learn to recognise her.

The chaffinch's call note, a sharp, loud *pink-pink*, is one of the most familiar sounds of the countryside, and the books will tell you that you can easily recognise the bird by that alone. But there is another remarkably like it which I have known to deceive even experienced naturalists. This is one of the many calls of the great tit. There is a slight difference which may be distinguished by a good ear, but it is so slight that it can only be suggested in syllables thus:—chaffinch *pink-pink*, great tit *ping-ping*. In the case of the great tit this double note is only part of the call, so if, when you hear it, you pause and listen for a moment or two the bird may presently give the full phrase, which is *ping-ping-zh-zh-zh-zh-zh*, and by that you will know that it is not the chaffinch.

The tits, however, are a very puzzling group to the beginner, a fact which makes them all the more interesting to any one with a spark of the explorer spirit in him. There are five common species, all of which frequent the lanes wherever there are trees. In winter they live in mixed flocks, and then you may often see all five species on one tree at the same time. They have a note that is common to them all, a shrill *see-see-see*, and two of them, the coal tit and the marsh tit, utter calls that are very much alike and at the same time bear a family resemblance to that of the great tit which I have already described. Only the owner of a good ear will be able to distinguish them from one another, but in order to learn them and the other calls and songs of these charming little birds, he must first be a very keen observer. The great tit is the largest of the five, and he may always be recognised by his black head, white cheeks, yellow under parts and black breast band. The coal tit and the marsh tit also have black heads, but they have no yellow feathers and no breast band. The former is a

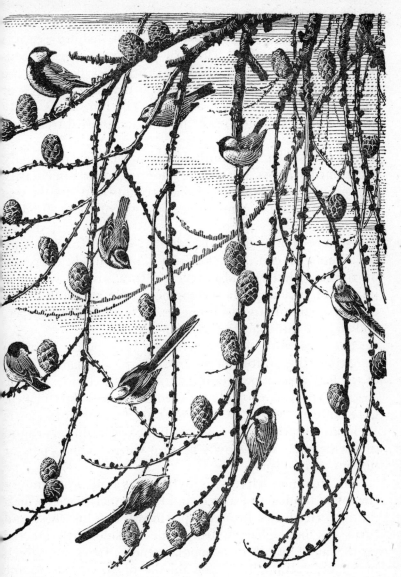

There you may often see five species of tit, **on** *one tree at the same time.*

greyish bird and the latter brownish, but this difference is not always noticeable. The coal tit, however, has a conspicuous white patch on the back of its black head. By the presence or absence of this mark you may know which of the two species you are watching. The blue tit is easily recognised by his blue head, and the long-tailed tit by his tail.

The chaffinch has another note which is not usually mentioned in books, but which, until it is known, may easily be confused with the call of the greenfinch. I myself was puzzled by it for a long time. The greenfinch is fond of sitting on the very top of a tree and uttering a long-drawn *br-r-r-eeze* at brief intervals, and may do this continuously for an hour on end. The chaffinch's note could be expressed by the same letters and is repeated in a similar way, but instead of perching on the topmost twig to shout it, he usually keeps among the branches. It is a harsher, sharper, and shorter call than the greenfinch's.

The greenfinch sings also from a high perch, a simple song consisting of four notes, *trit*, *trot*, *chum* and *breeze*, each of the first three repeated many times in succession and the *breeze* inserted occasionally between the phrases thus formed. Often in early spring he adds to it a very charming dance. He leaves his perch, and singing all the while, flutters round in a wide circle with slowly beating wings. This is part of his courtship display.

The chaffinch delivers his joyful lilt as a rule from among the lower branches of a tree, and his manner is well worth noting. He draws himself up, throws out his chest and turns his head sharply from side to side with all the pride and assurance of a popular tenor. His song, which has a beautiful trill in the middle of it, sounds to me like:

*What-what-what-what-d'you-r-r-r-r-really-
think-of-ME-now.*

The yellow-hammer, which is a close relative of the
finches, and can always be recognised by his bright yellow
canary-like head, sings a plaintive little ditty which is
commonly described as:

A-little-bit-of-bread-and-NO-cheese.

He delivers it from the top of the hedge or of some small
tree growing out of the hedge, and his manner is in keeping
with the character of his refrain, quiet and pensive like that
of a lady singing a sentimental ballad. The second last note
is so shrill that at a little distance it is hardly audible, but
often it is omitted altogether, and in other ways the ending
is varied. It is my belief that in some districts certain of
these variations are more frequently used than in others.

The hedge sparrow is another very common songster of
the hedge-top. He is a little brown bird with a blue-grey
head. The second part of his name, however, is a misnomer,
for he is not a sparrow, as you will see at once if you compare the two birds. The sparrow is a finch and has a short,
thick, hard beak excellently suited for cracking seeds. On
the other hand the hedge sparrow feeds upon insects and
has a comparatively long, thin, sharp, soft bill, a very
serviceable instrument for dealing with such luscious fare.
The distinction between the two is like that between a wire-
cutter and a pair of embroidery scissors.

Down among the lower branches of the hedge you may
see everywhere the little brown wren with his perky tail
cocked up at a rakish angle. Even when you do not see him
he will often announce his presence with his remarkably

loud call, which sounds like the winding-up of a large eight-day clock, or by his equally loud and resounding song, which half-way through is embellished with a brilliant trill, and suggests a bird of twice his size. As a rule he sings from a low and often hidden perch, but I have watched him giving his full performance while he was flying across the road from one hedge to the other.

Another bird that is given to skulking in the hedgerows is the whitethroat, one of our welcome summer visitors. He prefers the upper portion of the hedge and his call note is a harsh *churr*. When he sings, however, he throws discretion to the winds, and himself into the air, dancing up like a huge gnat to about ten feet above the hedge and down again. He is a small light brown bird.

Two of our most common birds, the song thrush and the blackbird, frequently nest in the hedgerows, but feed in the fields and sing from a high and prominent branch of a neighbouring tree. I have more than once, however, seen a thrush singing on the ground. The two species are closely related, and there is a family likeness in their songs, though is is quite easy to distinguish one from the other. The thrush's consists of a number of short phrases of one or more clearly defined notes. Each phrase is repeated quickly two or more times and is followed by a short pause. The blackbird sings longer phrases and slurs all his notes. He does not repeat like the thrush, but rather makes many variations of one phrase. This begins low with several rich and flute-like notes and ends high and shrilly, but as a whole it is the most beautiful of all our bird songs.

But though these two can be so easily recognised, there is a third which is often confused with one or the other. It is the song of the missel-thrush, which is a larger bird but has a speckled breast and is generally similar in colouring to the common thrush, and has the same habit of singing from a high perch. It has not the full quality of the blackbird's lower notes but lacks the shrill final ones. On the other hand its phrases are longer and not so varied as the thrush's. Most people are not aware of this bird's existence, but it is quite common and may be heard singing on any day from Christmas to the middle of May. It is fond of singing on stormy days, and from this peculiarity is known as the storm cock.

In the southern half of England, wherever the hedges are high and bushy you will see the turtle dove, which is another summer visitor. This bird feeds in the fields like the other pigeons but nests in the hedgerows. Its nest is most difficult to find, for it consists of a very slight platform of small dead twigs which are so loosely placed together that you can see the sky through them. The wonder is that the bird is able to rear its chicks on such a structure, or that the eggs are not thrown from it whenever a breeze sways the hedge. The turtle dove is much smaller than our other pigeons, and is light brown in colour. When it flies up, it spreads its tail and displays a broad white band at the tip. This bird does not coo like our more familiar species, but utters a continuous *turr-turr-turr* somewhat like the purring of the cat, and from this it gets its name.

The lanes have their tragedies as well as their joys and beauties, and at any moment you may see there a vision of sudden death. You may be watching a number of small birds flitting about the hedgerow feeding, singing, playing, quarrelling, or fetching food for their young, when, without warning, a large bird will flash swiftly round a bend, snatch one of them in its talons and fly off with it, amid a wild outcry of excited chattering from all the other birds in the immediate neighbourhood. This is the sparrow hawk.

If you are quick enough to notice it you will recognise it by its blue-grey back, or its brown breast barred with black. It is not always successful, and in that event it may alight on the hedge or a telegraph wire and so give you a good view of its form and plumage. But whether it does or not the incident will demonstrate to you the value of the alarm call to birds in general. The moment one of them spies the approaching terror it utters its own warning note, and this is recognised and the signal is repeated and so passed on by each species in its own way, every individual at the same moment scurrying to shelter.

You may sometimes see the situation reversed, the sparrow hawk, terrified, hiding in some bush while a company of tits or other feathered mites shriek the direst threats at it. This shows that the hawks are not wanton destroyers, but kill only when they are hungry. When they have had a good meal they are not only harmless, but are not capable of defending themselves against weaker birds which they could scatter to the winds by a simple demonstration of force. It also shows that the small birds are able to recognise their enemy, apart from his appearance when he is attacking, and that they know when they are safe.

The hedges themselves are full of interest apart from the creatures that shelter or feed in them. A garden hedge usually consists of one plant which is so pruned and trained that it loses all its character. But in the lanes and the open country where they are allowed to run wild, the hedges are made up of a variety of plants each of which has a character and habits of its own.

In February, or even as early as January, the hazel brings life into the hedgerows by unfurling its beautiful yellow tassels, which wave gaily with every breath of air. These are the male flowers of the plant. Presently they wither away, and where they have been you need not expect to find nuts. But on other parts of the same bush another kind of flower is in bloom at the same time. It is so inconspicuous, however, that it must be looked for. If you examine the larger leaf buds you will see, protruding from the tips of some, two or three tiny crimson threads. These are the flowers which will later develop into tempting hazel nuts. But they must first be fertilised by the male flowers. You may see for yourself how this is done. Shake the tassels and a little cloud of fine dust will break from them. This dust floats on the air till some of it settles on the tiny red flowers, and at that moment the process begins which ends with the shedding of the ripe nut in September.

The first of the hedge bushes to put forth leaves is the elder tree. You may know this plant easily by the fact that its twigs are angular and their hollow centres are filled with light pith, which can easily be removed if you wish to make pea-shooters. Its leaves are large with five, seven, or nine narrow leaflets with toothed edges. But though this tree is in leaf so early, it does not blossom till June. Then you may know it by its large, flat bunches of white flowers which have a heavy, unpleasant odour. And again in autumn you will see, where these bunches have been, similar bunches of small black berries.

Two other hedge bushes are closely related to the elder, though to the ordinary observer they are as different from it as possible. In spring you may recognise the wayfaring tree by its peculiar buds. On some of its twigs there are large round button-shaped buds, each with a long pointed bud sticking up on either side of it like asses' ears. The latter are leaf buds, and they unfold into large more or less oval leaves, which seem to be covered with dust, but are really coated with fine hairs. The button buds expand in

May into flat roundish bunches of small white flowers, which later develop into berries which are first green, then orange, then bright red, and finally glossy black. These berries may be recognised by the fact that they are egg-shaped and are grown upright instead of hanging.

The guelder rose is not a rose but a member of the elder family. Its leaves are large, but they have three pointed lobes, each of which has toothed edges. Its flowers, however, are much the most interesting feature of the plant. They appear in June and July, and like those of the elder and the wayfaring tree, they are small and white and are grown in large flat bunches. But they differ in this, that the outer ring of blossoms are all three times as large as the rest. When these are examined they are found to be incapable of producing seed. They are grown for the sole purpose of attracting attention to their less conspicuous sisters. The small flowers of the inner rings develop later into round, drooping, bright red berries.

Two common hedgerow plants that are often confused by beginners are the privet and the dogwood. The privet is the bush that is so frequently used to form garden hedges. You may know it by its small, narrow, almost oval, smooth leaves. The dogwood has similar leaves, but they are more rounded and their veins all curve towards the tip. In May or June the privet produces large upright pyramidal bunches of white flowers. The dogwood blossoms in June, and its flowers which may be recognised by their four long, sharply pointed petals, grow in small round, flat bunches. The berries that develop from these flowers are black when they ripen in autumn, and of course they are grouped in a similar fashion. But then the leaves are the best distinction between the two plants. The privet is almost evergreen, but the dogwood leaves change to beautiful dark crimson and purple shades before they fall.

The hawthorn is the commonest of all our hedge plants. Its other name, May, refers to its habit of blossoming in the month of May. It is one of the earliest of our bushes to come into leaf, its bursting buds being known in March by the village children as bread and cheese. Its cousin, the blackthorn, reverses this practice. Early in April it produces a gay display of white flowers while most of its neighbours are leafless, and its own leaves do not appear until several weeks later. You should note that whereas the blackthorn blossoms are grown singly or in pairs, those of the haw-thorn are grouped in large, closely-packed bunches, and whereas the leaves of the blackthorn are single-pointed, those of the hawthorn have five or seven fingers, or, more correctly, rounded lobes.

Now, while these plants are related to each other, they belong to the rose family which also includes the bramble, so it is easy to compare them also with the roses and brambles which scramble over or near them. As all these plants blossom at different seasons, it is not possible to examine their flowers side by side, but if you bear in mind the form and character of the wild rose while you are looking at any of the other three, you will not fail to see in all of them a strong family likeness. Then when autumn comes, you will be astonished to find how extraordinarily diverse are the fruits they produce. The sloe or wild plum, which is black, with a beautiful purple bloom on it, is the fruit of the blackthorn. How different that is in form, colour and contents from the rich red hip of the rose! And again, how both of them differ from the dark red haws of the hawthorn, and from the blackberry which is the fruit of the bramble.

Then notice the difference between the thorns of the thorn bushes and those of the rose and the bramble. The former are just short, straight twigs that are grown without leaves and are sharply pointed to wound the mouths of browsing animals. The latter are special growths and are curved at the point like the claws of a cat. They are also capable of wounding, but they serve another purpose as well. Their owners both produce long thin branches which are not strong enough to support themselves but must lean on something else. For this purpose they find hedges very convenient, and their claw-like thorns help to give them a hold while they scramble up and over.

A number of other plants utilise the hedgerows as a means by which they can raise themselves in the world. They are not scramblers but true climbers, and they achieve their end in various ways. For example the honeysuckle, which is one of the commonest, twines its long lithe stem round the branches of the hedge, and always does so in the direction followed by the hands of the clock, that is, from left to right.

The honeysuckle is one of the first plants to open its leaves in spring. Indeed on mild days in December you may often see honeysuckle in leaf. The reason for this is that the plant has no true buds. Its young leaves are not protected by warm bud scales, and so at the first touch of mildness in the air they come out like the gnats to enjoy the sun. Consequently they are often nipped by frost.

The honeysuckle blossom is also very interesting. It consists of a long tube, and, as every one knows, it has a very sweet scent. You will notice, however, that the scent is strongest in the evening, and there is a very good reason for this. The plant always opens its blossoms first in the evening. This it does for the purpose of attracting night-

The plant always opens its blossoms first in the evening.

flying moths, which have tongues that are long enough to reach its honey and so are well fitted to carry its fertilising pollen from one blossom to another.

Another very common climber is the black bryony, which may be recognised easily by its large heart-shaped leaves. This plant climbs in the same manner as the honey-suckle, but its sensitiveness is so astonishing that it almost seems to think. It has an uncanny sense of the exact position of any upright within its range, and if it cannot reach this with one of its limp stems, it will twist several of them together and so gain strength enough to bridge even con-siderable gaps. If you care to watch, you may see the tip of one of its climbing stalks turn a complete circle in less than three hours.

In autumn the leaves of the black bryony become a rich dark bronze, and its strings of berries, which are first green, then orange and finally red, give a brilliant touch of colour to the hedgerows.

Whenever you meet with the large convolvulus, you should compare it if possible with the honeysuckle or the black bryony. You may know it at once by its spear-shaped leaves and by its large white trumpet-like flowers. At any rate you should note that it twines in the opposite direction to them, that is, starting from twelve o'clock it travels from right to left.

The wild clematis, or travellers' joy, or old man's beard is a species of buttercup with a lofty ambition. It not only climbs up the hedge but often attains a high position on a tree above it. The plant is best known as it appears in autumn when its seeds, each with a long white feather attached to it, cover great patches of the hedge in a manner that at first sight suggests snow. But it is also interesting in July because it is then starred with little greenish white flowers. It is quite easy to identify because it climbs, not by twining but by twisting the stalks of its leaves round twigs.

The tufted vetch is a kind of pea with long bunches of small blue flowers, which may be known by the similarity of their form to that of the familiar sweet pea. Its leaf consists of a long stalk with a number of little oval leaflets arranged in pairs on it, but with the tip split up into three thread-like tendrils. The plant climbs by twisting these tendrils round any support it can find.

The white bryony, in spite of its name, is not related in any way to the black bryony. It is a member of the melon or marrow family and has large five-fingered leaves, whereas the black bryony belongs to the yam tribe. There is little to choose, however, between the two plants in the keenness of their instinct for what will best serve their purpose. I have often been astonished at the certainty with which the main stem of both makes for the nearest support though it may be several yards away.

Instead of twining, the white bryony sends out special tendrils. These are not part of the leaf stalk, but are separate organs, and they are extremely sensitive, as much so as the tips of the black bryony stems. When they touch a support they immediately curl round it, and then they pull in the slack by twisting themselves up into a spring. By this means they raise the trailing stem and enable it to reach up farther, but they actually do the work of a spring, for when the support is shaken by the wind their twisted portion stretches and absorbs the strain, and so they are saved from damage whereas the main stem is insured against loss of support.

Then there is the ivy, which does not climb by twining its stem nor by twisting tendrils, but gains support by sending out little rootlets from the back of its stems and twigs. These take hold of the trunks and branches of the hedge bushes and so enable the plant to mount higher and higher. They are not real roots, however, for they do not draw sap from the supporting bush. They are just suckers and, as every one knows, they are as well able to grip a barren wall as a growing tree.

Unlike all our other wild plants the ivy flowers in autumn and winter, and fruits in spring. The flower produces a large flow of honey which is very attractive to moths. So if you care to go out after dark in September and October with a lantern, you may see on them moths of many species, too many to mention here.

The berries are black when they are ripe, and they provide food for birds when the autumn fruits are long gone, and the spring supplies of fresh food are not yet plentiful.

One more conspicuous feature of the hedgerow is the beautiful red bunch of what looks like moss that grows so frequently on the wild rose and is known as Robin's pincushion. This is not a normal growth; it is really a gall, and it is caused by a tiny member of the wasp family. The adult wasp emerges in spring and lays her eggs in a rose bud with the result that, when the bud expands, it produces this mossy structure instead of leaves. The grubs live inside this ball of moss, sucking the juices of the plant till they are full grown, and then remaining there in the chrysalis state until it is time for the complete insect to emerge. If you care to cut one of these pincushions in two you may learn how they work, or if you take one home in autumn and keep it in a box you may see the mature wasp when it emerges next spring.

CHAPTER THREE

THE WOODS

IN the woods we meet with the most charming of all our four-footed animals, the little red squirrel. He is also one of the very few that we may expect to find abroad during the day. As he lives and moves and feeds very largely among the tree tops and can quickly find refuge there if he happens to be alarmed when he is on the ground, he has no need to avoid the sunlight, so he boldly comes out and enjoys his life by day and sleeps cosily in his secret retreat by night. But he is none the less wary, so if you are not careful you may tramp through the woods for a whole day and see no sign of him whatever, or at best only a fleeting glimpse of him before he vanishes as if by magic. Sounds and movements are his surest signals of danger, so if you wish to study him at close quarters, you must be ready the moment you spy him to stop and remain still and silent until his fears have been allayed. Other animals crouch when they are aware of an enemy's approach, but the favourite trick of the squirrel, if he is surprised when he is on the ground, is to climb a few feet up the trunk of a tree on the side farthest away from the intruder, and to cling there with legs wide spread and head, body and tail pressed close to the bark. There he will remain till the clumsy stroller has passed on out of sight and earshot, peeping anxiously round the tree to watch him go, and then he will relax and proceed with his search for food. But if you have stopped in time and can keep still, you may presently have the satisfaction of watching him open a nut or strip a pine cone, both very interesting operations.

He will sit up on his haunches either on the ground, on a stump or on a branch, with his tail gracefully curled over his back, and holding the hazel nut in his forepaws with the narrow end uppermost, will nibble off the tip. That done it is a matter of moments only for him to slip his strong incisor teeth into the hole he has made and split the shell in half. Or, if his treasure is a pine cone he will hold it horizontally between his forepaws, one paw on each end, and twisting it round rapidly away from him, will nip off the scales with his sharp teeth as quickly and neatly as if he were a skilled mechanic working a lathe. Or again he will go to the very top of a high branch, and holding there by his hind paws will reach down to secure some cone or bud that has taken his fancy. Or if it is autumn and he is searching among the fallen leaves for nuts, you may see him scrape a little hole in the ground, deposit his treasure there and cover it up, or carry it to some hole in a tree where he is laying by a store for the winter.

It is worth while sometimes to allow him to know that

you have seen him. He will then become very angry, will climb to a fork of a tree and peeping over at you, will scold you roundly with his familiar note, *chuck-chuck-chuck*. Then if you persist in standing there and looking at him he will show you how easily he can escape from you by passing from tree to tree without ever coming to the ground, finding with masterly skill the point at which they are most narrowly separated from one another, springing easily across the intervening space and then passing by the quickest branch route to the leap that will take him to the next tree and so on.

Besides his *chuck* note, he has another which he uses when he is alarmed. It sounds like *skee-ow-w-w*.

Now, though he is called the red squirrel, it is well to know that he is not always red. This is only his summer colour, but at that time he does not change the fur on his tail and his ear tufts. These become paler and more ragged as the summer advances, and then in August and September he moults his whole coat and replaces it with a new one for the winter. This is thick and warm and is brown mixed with grey. The tip of the tail soon begins to bleach and, long before the red summer coat is put on again in May, the whole tail and the ear tufts are quite flaxen, and are already beginning to thin.

The fox and the badger are also denizens of the wood. You may by chance catch a fleeting glimpse of a fox by day, or if you happen to know a fox's den and can hide yourself in its vicinity, you may watch the cubs come out and play before it. If you wish to see a badger, however, you must find his burrow, station yourself near it about dusk and wait for him to emerge. If he scents you he will not venture forth, so you must be careful to hide on the leeward side of his home.

There are many interesting birds in the woods. Tits thrushes and others that are common in the hedgerows and fields may be found there too, but a number of species, such as the woodpeckers for example, find most of their living in the wood, though they may frequently be seen on isolated trees in fields or gardens.

Three species of woodpecker live with us all the year round. The commonest is the green woodpecker, which is also the largest. You cannot help knowing when he is in your neighbourhood, for he shouts the information to all with ears to hear in his loud laughing call. From this call he has been named the yaffle. It sounds like *yah-yah-yah-yah yah*, each repeated on a lower note than the one before it.

You may recognise the bird on the wing by his large head and long heavy bill and his short stubby tail, and also by his peculiar undulating flight. When he is flying away from you his most conspicuous feature is a greenish yellow patch on the lower part of his back.

Now, the woodpecker is specially adapted for climbing trees. He has four toes on each foot, two in front and two behind, and these enable him to take a firm grip on the bark and either to cling there or to run up or down trunk or branch. In this he is aided by his short tail, the feathers of which are strong and, when pressed against the tree, help to support him. With his long, strong bill he taps the tree and, when the sound tells him that a grub lies within, he chisels off the bark and with his long sticky tongue draws his victim forth. He also cuts with his bill the deep hole in the tree in which the eggs are laid and the young reared You may frequently see such holes in the trunks or large branches of trees which show any signs of decay, and old woodpecker trees are pitted all over with little workings from which the birds have taken grubs.

The greater spotted woodpecker is not quite so large as the green woodpecker, but in colour he is black with white markings on his wings and on the side of his head, and bright crimson on the nape of his neck and underneath, on the hind part of his body. His mate is similar, but does not have the crimson on her neck. Their call is a single note which sounds like *geck*.

The lesser spotted woodpecker is much smaller. He is just about the size of a sparrow, but similar in form and in habits to his larger relatives. He has much white on his back as well as on his wings and head, but no crimson on his under parts or his nape though he has a bright patch on his crown.

His call consists of one clear, high note repeated five or six times. It is impossible to give a better description of it than that, and it has to be heard and learnt, otherwise it may be confused with calls of two other birds, the wryneck and the nuthatch.

But he has another means of expressing himself or attracting the attention of his mate. This is known as drumming, and consists in striking a branch repeatedly in such a way that it gives forth a resounding note, like the roll of a kettle-drum, which can best be described as *r-r-r-r-r-r-r-r-r-r*. The greater spotted woodpecker also does this, and I am convinced that I have heard the green woodpecker do it too. Here is one of the problems of nature that you might help to solve.

Both the spotted woodpeckers keep strictly to the trees. The green woodpecker, however, picks up his living very largely on the ground. He has found that good meals are to be got easily by attacking ants' nests.

The wryneck is a distant relative of the woodpeckers, and he is only a summer visitor to this country. He has the same kind of feet as the woodpeckers, but he seldom climbs trees. Consequently he does not use his tail as a support, and it is interesting therefore to know that his tail feathers are not stiff. He alights on the branches, but instead of sitting on them crosswise with his toes gripping round them he faces along them. He is rather larger than the lesser spotted woodpecker, and his plumage is brown speckled with light and dark markings which, however, are not obvious except at fairly close quarters. He has a peculiar habit of twisting his neck, and from this he has been given his name. He is also known as the cuckoo's mate because he arrives in April about the same time as that bird.

His call is a single note uttered five or more times in quick succession. It is somewhat like the lesser spotted woodpecker's, but its distinctive feature is a slight huskiness as if the bird had a cold. In fact once this note is heard and identified it cannot be mistaken for any other.

The nuthatch is a perching bird and is not related to the woodpeckers, but he climbs as well as the best of them, and without the aid of his tail. He can run up or down a tree, round a branch or sideways along it with equal facility, but he frequently visits the smaller twigs after the manner of a tit. He has a strong, straight, sharp bill with which he digs grubs from their lairs, but in autumn and winter he takes nuts and acorns, fixes them in some crevice on a branch, hammers them with his bill till he smashes the shell, and then eats the contents. Hence his name.

He is a handsome little bird, slate-blue above and buff and chestnut underneath, and with a conspicuous black mark running from his bill across the side of his head.

He has several calls. The commonest of them is a clear double note like *whit-whit*. In spring, however, he utters another like *pwee-ah* which may be confused with certain notes of the song thrush, and yet another so like that of the lesser spotted woodpecker that only an experienced ear can tell the difference.

Another little climber is the tree creeper. He is also a percher, but he never perches. He has become so devoted to climbing that even when he roosts he just clings to the side of a tree like a woodpecker. That being so, it is interesting to note that he uses his tail as a support after the manner of a woodpecker, and consequently his tail feathers have become stiff and strong. He has a long curved bill with which he is able to search the crannies of bark for insects, spiders and so on.

He is a little brown bird with white under parts, and his habit is to begin at the foot of a tree, climb up the trunk and one of the larger branches, then drop to the bottom of another tree and begin over again. Whenever you see a company of tits in a wood in winter it will be worth your while to look round for a tree creeper also, for these birds consort after the nesting season.

The books will tell you that the call and song of the tree creeper are so shrill as to be inaudible to some people. The truth is that he is a very silent bird, but when you once know his call you need never miss it unless you are deaf, and his song is as loud and clear as that of any warbler, but it is very seldom sung. It consists of three phrases which sound like *te-te-tree*, *te-te-tree*, *te-te-tree-tree-tree-tree-tree*. The first eight syllables are on one high note, but the last five form a descending scale.

The jay and the magpie are handsome members of the crow family which are partial to woodlands. You may consider yourself a skilled woodsman if you can get near enough to a jay to see the details of his beautiful plumage, especially the wonderful blue feathers of his wings. His

harsh cry, however, which suggests his name, is unmistake
able, and as he flies away from you, he will give you a
momentary vision of a white rump with a reddish-brown
back above it and a dark tail below it. His flight is un
dulating with a characteristic uncertainty which almos
suggests weakness. You will recognise the magpie by hi
bold black and white plumage and long black tail, and b
his loud chattering call.

In copses and in woods where there is much undergrowth
you may hear the nightingale from April to June. He, how
ever, has this peculiarity that, whereas you may find him
plentiful in some districts, he may be altogether unknown
only a mile or two away, and you may not meet with him
again for ten or twenty miles.

When he sings he is usually hidden among the bushes
and as a rule, he prefers a perch within a few feet of th
ground. If you live in a nightingale district you may easil
learn his song because of the fact that he sings by nigh
when he has no competitors. But you may also hear him
singing by day, often only a snatch or two, but sometime
his full song. There is this to be noted about the song, tha
it consists of a series of separate phrases with a short paus
after each. This is the manner of the thrush, and th
nightingale belongs to the thrush family.

There are several other good singers of the woodland
but they belong to quite a different family. They are th
warblers, all of them small birds of about five to six inche
in length, roughly about the size of a sparrow. The com
monest of them is the willow warbler, a little olive gree
bird with a yellow breast and a yellow stripe over the ey
This description, however, would suit two other warbler
namely the chiff-chaff and the wood warbler, and for th
average observer their songs are the best means of distin

guishing the three. The willow warbler's is a very sweet phrase of a dozen or more notes in a descending scale as if it were singing the word "we" again and again. The chiff-chaff's is just the two syllables of his name repeated many times, with an occasional variation such as *chiff-chaff-chaff* or *chiff-chiff-chaff*. The wood warbler is much rarer than the others, and prefers the tall trees of the wood, especially beech trees. There he sits, not on the tree tops, but on a high bough and sings his very distinctive song which sounds like *Tee-Tee-Tee-Tee t-t-t-t-t-t-trrrree*.

The blackcap and the garden warbler are also lovers of the wood, but like the nightingale they prefer the bushy undergrowth and there they are more often heard than seen. Their songs are both very beautiful, but they are so remarkably similar that even experts are often unable to say which is which. As a matter of fact there is a very distinct difference between the two which can be quite simply described. Both have rich full fluty notes similar to the blackbird's, but the blackcap's are all soft and slurred, whereas there is a marked rolling in the garden warbler's which suggests that he is pronouncing his r's like a Scotsman.

Whenever you come upon a group of pine or fir trees you should listen and look for the little golden-crested wren. It is our smallest bird and it is often difficult to see because of its restless tit-like activity. But if you get a near view of it you will notice that it is olive green, has two white bars on its wings and a bright golden patch on the crown of its head. Its song is so light that it is almost a whisper. The following gives a good idea of it: *Ithywee-ithywee-ithywee-chi-chi-chirrupy-wee*. You must listen carefully if you wish to hear the latter half.

Another very interesting bird of the woods is the nightjar. He is a large bird, and you may sometimes see him by day if you happen to disturb him. But as a rule he remains hidden on the ground till about dusk, and he is specially fond of situations where the floor of the wood is covered with bracken. I have often noticed that he begins to call just about the time when the first of the night moths appear. If you go into the woods then, you may approach quite close to him by simply following the sound of his remarkable churring call. You will find him in some comparatively open part of the wood, and you will notice that like the wryneck, he sits along the branch not across it. Presently he will leave his perch and flit slowly across an open space clapping his wings smartly over his back. This clapping seems to be one of his signals to his mate. Then he will silently hawk to and fro, hovering every now and then with tail depressed as he pauses to capture some fluttering moth.

Watching the nightjar thus at work in the heart of a wood after dusk is a romantic experience which every true lover of nature should enjoy at least once. If at the same time you care to "sugar" some of the trees and visit them a little later with a lantern, you will be astonished at the number of moths of many species that flit through the woodland glades at night though you may see none in the same place during the day. Moths are able to hide themselves very cleverly, but if you keep a sharp look-out on the trunks of the trees as you pass, you may often see one resting there and trusting for protection to the similarity of its colouring to that of the bark.

The best time to make yourself familiar with the trees is summer, for then their leaves afford a very simple means of identification. Some leaves are a little puzzling at first. For example those of the beech, the elm and the hornbeam are similar in size and shape, but if you put them side by side their differences will at once be apparent. The most obvious is that the elm has toothed edges, the hornbeam's has a number of little teeth between larger ones, and the beech's has no teeth but only slightly irregular margins.

You should note that the structure of a tree is influenced considerably by the size of its leaves, just as the thickness of a cable depends on the weight it has to support. Beech leaves, for example, are on the whole larger than hornbeam and elm than beech, and consequently if you were to compare shoots of the three, say at a point behind the last six leaves, you would find that the elm was the stoutest and the hornbeam the thinnest. The differences between them are very slight, but if you compare any of them with the lime, the ash, and the chestnut in this order, you will see there is a considerable increase in the thickness of the twig in proportion to the size of the leaf. You should note that the ash leaf consists of a long stalk with many leaflets on each side and one at the tip, and that the chestnut leaf has five or more large leaflets which are spread out like the fingers of an open hand.

Again, leaves are the organs by which plants are able to utilise the rays of the sun in order to carry on the processes on which their growth depends. So they are displayed with the object of catching the greatest possible amount of sunlight, and each tree has dealt with this problem in its own way. The most successful in this respect is the beech, for its leaves are so arranged that not enough sunlight can pass between them to enable other plants to live underneath. Consequently there is no interesting undergrowth in a beech wood.

You will notice that the shoots of the beech are somewhat zig-zag in shape, the buds appearing at the angles and the leaves being directed forward in such a way that very little space is left between their margins and the side of the twig. The leaves of the elm are attached more or less at right angles to the twig. In both cases the leaves are produced one on each side of the twig alternately. The sycamore and the horse chestnut grow their long-stalked, hand-like leaves in pairs, each pair at right angles to the one above or below it, the lowest ones having the longest stalks and the highest the shortest, and the whole shoot thus forming a kind of umbrella.

Each tree also has its own method of flowering and producing seed. The elm and the ash, for example, both flower before their foliage appears, the oak catkins tumble out of the leaf buds as soon as they open. The birch, which you may always recognise by its white bark, has special buds for its pollen catkins and these when they open hang downwards, but the seeding flowers appear from the leaf buds and stand upright. The flower buds of the horse chestnut grow from certain leaf buds and they themselves open in the latter part of May, and the lime bursts into blossom in July long after its leaves have lost their first freshness.

The elm fruits drop about the time the leaves appear. Each is carried more or less in the centre of a little aeroplane. The ash fruit which falls in autumn is also carried by a plane, which, however, is long, narrow and pointed. The sycamore seeds are twins, but each has a wing of its own, so when they drop they work in consort and twirl away from their parent. Each hornbeam nut has a broad three-fingered sail, and every little bunch of lime fruits is attached to a long sword-shaped one. The oak produces its acorns openly, each in a little cup, and the beech hides its brown three-cornered nuts in a very hard, bristly case until they are ripe.

The flower buds of the horse-chestnut grow from certain leaf buds.

Even in the withering and discarding of its leaves each tree has it sown special characteristics. The beech leaves change to rich reds and browns, but the elm leaves become golden yellow. Most leaves wither from the margins inwards till only the veins remain green, but the veins of the sycamore become rich blood red. These and other trees soon appear ragged when their leaves begin to fall because those at the tips drop first, but the lime and the poplars retain their summer outlines to the end because their inner leaves go first and the outermost ones last.

And when at length the trees are bare, they may each be recognised by their characteristic branching or by their bark or buds. The beech has a broomlike appearance, the elm a bushy top. The larger branches of the oak often strike out at right angles to the trunk, a sure sign of great strength, and the smaller ones are much twisted. You may know the horse chestnut by its thick, clumsy twigs, the ash by its grey bark and black buds, and so on.

The difference between these deciduous trees and the evergreens is that the latter retain their leaves for several seasons instead of only for one. Quantities of ivy leaves, for example, are shed every summer. Holly leaves live for about four years, pine needles for three as a rule, and fir needles for eight or more.

Green foliage in mid-winter must be a great temptation to browsing animals, so the holly protects its leaves with spines. You will notice that these spines are not horizontal, but point alternately upwards and downwards as if the tree understood that the enemy was a two-jawed monster.

The simplest distinction between a pine and a fir is the fact that fir needles are single and are arranged spirally round the twigs, whereas pine needles are in tufts of two, three or five. Those of the common Scots pine grow in pairs. The larch belongs to the same family, but it grows its needles in tufts of more than five, and sheds them in autumn.

Many well-known flowers carpet the floor of the woods —wood anemone, primrose, bluebell, woodruff and so on— but among them there are several that are specially interesting. Take the primrose for example. This species has two kinds of blossom and they are grown on separate plants. One with a pale green pinhead or seed-making flower in the mouth of its tube is called the pin-eyed, and the other with a circle of five pollen flowers is known as the thrum-eyed. Half-way down inside the tube of the pin-eyed there is a circle of pollen flowers, and at the same depth inside the tube of the thrum-eyed there is the pinhead of a seed-making flower. So when an insect with a tongue long enough to reach the honey visits one kind, it carries dust from the pollen flowers on that part of its proboscis which will come in contact with the seed-making flower of the other kind.

Now, strange to tell, very few insects visit the primrose. When you think of the scarcity of honey flowers in the first half of April and how precious they must be to insects at that early season, it is astonishing to learn that bees pass by the primrose. Formerly it was believed that moths visited its blossoms after dark, and some writers still assert this though they do not go out to see for themselves. I have examined primrose banks at night and not found moths on the blossoms, but as these insects are very uncertain creatures more records are needed. There is a problem for you to solve.

However, on any sunny day in April you may see both the brimstone butterfly and the bee-fly sucking honey from the primrose. You cannot mistake the male brimstone because his colour is primrose. The female is much paler in shade and at a little distance may seem to be white, but at close quarters you may recognise her by the orange spot in the middle of her wings. The bee-fly resembles the bumble bee both in form and in the possession of a furry coat. But it has only two wings, and when it alights it keeps them outstretched, whereas the bee has four and folds them over her back. The bee-fly also has a long beak which cannot be withdrawn like the proboscis of the bee.

The bugle which is blue, the archangel which is bright yellow, and the foxglove are all so formed that they can be fertilised only by bumble bees. The bugle and the archangel have two lips, the lower one expanded to offer a hospitable landing-place to the bee, and the upper one arched like a hood. Under this canopy you will find the two kinds of flower. They are placed there so that they may be brushed by the furry back of the bee. The foxglove is different in shape, but the lower half of its bell protrudes and so forms a platform, and the flowers are hidden under the upper half where they are swept by the bee's fur as she goes in to reach the honey.

The little wood sorrel is one of our most wonderful plants. Its leaves sleep as well as its flowers. They consist of three leaflets which are fixed at the top of an upright stalk, and they are so sensitive to light that they droop round it like a closed umbrella at dusk and also in very bright sunshine, but in the morning, and so long as it is not subjected to brilliant light in the hottest part of the day, they are outspread to the sun's rays from whatever angle they may be striking through the wood.

When its delicate white flowers wither their stalks droop till the heads are hidden among the leaves, but when the seeds are ripening, they rise again, and the reason for this second action is very interesting. By a sudden stripping of their covering the seeds are shot out forcibly and as, owing to the upright position of the stalk, they are held well above the leaves and so have a clear space in which to travel, they fly to a distance of several feet.

Sometime later, however, the plant produces other flowers which never emerge from the bud, but which nevertheless develop seed. They are borne on much shorter stalks, which bend down and bury the ripe seed among the moss or leafage that covers the ground.

The dog violet also grows similar closed flowers in summer, but strange to tell, it depends on them almost entirely to provide seeds for next year. Its millions of beautiful spring blossoms are nearly all wasted. No satisfactory explanation has ever been made of this astonishing fact. Blue is the most attractive of all colours to a bee. The violet is blue, and it is so wonderfully contrived that when bees are sucking honey with their long tongues from the horn at the back of the flower, their heads must be dusted with pollen which should therefore be carried to the next blossom and so on. But nevertheless these flowers are very seldom fertilised. Our greatest naturalist, Darwin, suggested that the closed summer flowers were grown for economy. But how can it be economical to manufacture an article for a pound if you always waste a million pounds before you begin? Can it be that the pollen is too dry and drops from the bee's head before she reaches the next blossom? Or is there some still better explanation? Here is an opportunity for some enthusiastic young nature lover.

CHAPTER FOUR

COMMONS

THE stoat is a hunter. He preys upon rabbits, rats, mice, birds, and even squirrels, so he may be seen wherever these creatures are to be found. He is very wary. I have seen him pause suddenly and listen when his sharp ears caught the click of a gate a hundred yards away. So you are not likely to meet him except by chance. But many times while I have been sitting or standing in the more open part of a wood waiting for or observing other creatures, a stoat has come to within a few feet of me before discovering me, and I have actually watched one at close quarters climb a tall tree and come down again. I was very much impressed then by the difference between his method and that of the squirrel. The stoat ascends slowly hand over hand, taking advantage of any twigs or small branches that may be growing from the trunk, drawing himself up on them and then proceeding as before, but the squirrel mounts quickly in a series of bounds.

The stoat has a narrow, snake-like body about a foot long. His tail adds from four to six inches to his length but looks stubby compared to the rest. His legs are very short, and his whole structure is admirably adapted for following his prey into its burrow. He can run at a good pace in spite of the shortness of his legs, but as a rule he progresses by a series of peculiar long leaps, zig-zagging as he goes either to give himself the greatest possible chance of picking up the trail of some likely prey or, as I have often thought, for the purpose of breaking his own, for he has a very strong odour.

His colour is reddish brown above and white underneath, but the tip of his tail is black. In northern or mountainous parts of the country where there is much snow, his whole coat becomes white in winter with the exception of the black part of his tail. He is then known as the ermine. In the south he changes only partially or not at all.

The weasel is about half the size of the stoat, and is similar in colouring except that the tip of his tail is not black. His habits are also similar, only he feeds more on small animals, mice, voles, and young rats and the smaller birds. He is a much more agile climber than the stoat, and can run up a tree quite easily. Like the stoat, he makes his nest in holes in old walls, banks, or trees.

Both animals are very playful when they are at home and not engaged in the serious affairs of life. It is a charming sight to see a family of young ones rolling, tumbling and somersaulting over each other. This game is sometimes practised by an adult as a clever means of obtaining a meal.

If you hear a number of birds making a great outcry in a thicket or among the scrub of a common, you may be almost sure that their alarm is caused by the presence of a stoat. Be on the alert then, for you may see a very wonderful incident. The stoat follows his four-footed prey by scent, but he often captures birds by turning somersaults before them and so fascinating them or playing upon their curiosity that he is able to approach and pounce upon them before they realise their danger.

On open commons away from trees, one of the most plentiful birds is the meadow-pipit, a little brown bird with a speckled breast, somewhat resembling a lark but rather smaller. Unlike his cousin, the tree-pipit, this species remains with us all the year round. He is easily recognised by having a white feather on each side of his tail and by his frequently repeated call which is a shrill *sip-sip-sip*. In spring and summer he strings this note into a kind of song which he utters while he is mounting to thirty or forty feet in the air, and then planing down with outstretched wings either to the ground or to a low spray of gorse. Near the end he introduces some other notes, which you may easily miss, but the song is never so brilliant as the tree-pipit's.

While you are threading your way among the gorse, your ear may catch an oft-repeated sharp sound as if two hard stones were being struck together. If you turn your eyes in the direction from which it comes, you will see sitting on the top of a bush one of our handsomest birds. He is the stone-chat. You will recognise him by his black upper parts which are broken by conspicuous white patches on the neck, the wings and the upper part of the tail, and by his red breast. Presently he will drop to the ground to feed, but before long he will be back on his perch again calling *whit-chat* as before. In these actions and also in his habit of flicking his wings and tail frequently as he calls, there is something that reminds you of the robin.

The stone-chat lives with us all the year round, but he has a cousin called the whin-chat which is only a summer visitor. In spite of its name you are more likely to find this bird in grassy meadows than on gorsy commons, but you may meet with it there also. Both birds frequent railway embankments, and as they have similar calls, it is important to be able to distinguish them. The whin-chat also has white on neck, wings and tail, but his upper parts are streaky brown and his breast is buff not red. The feature, however, by which you will know him most readily is a broad white stripe above the eye.

The linnet, whose praises have been sung by the poets, is also an inhabitant of gorsy commons. He is a somewhat plain little bird. His general colouring is brown, but in spring and summer he has a crimson patch on his crown and on his breast. This crimson disappears in autumn, reappears gradually in spring and is at its best in July.

At all seasons the linnet is fond of company. In winter he lives in flocks, and you may often see one of these flocks sitting on a tree and singing a very pleasing little twittering chorus. In spring, of course, each pair has its own part of the common where the nest is hidden, and then you may hear the famous song, which the cock sings from a spray of gorse, or from a neighbouring tree, or while fluttering in the air. While they are not otherwise engaged, however, the cocks have a habit of sitting on the tops of the gorse bushes and calling to each other with two plaintive notes which sound like *tew-ee*.

Where there are hawthorn bushes on the common, you should look out for the red-backed shrike or butcher bird. His favourite perch is the top of a thorn bush. The features by which you will know him are his bluish grey head which has a bold black stripe on each side, and his bright chestnut back. He will sit on his bush-top silently for a time, or perhaps uttering occasionally his sharp call-note *chack*, then suddenly will take a short flight and capture an insect on the wing and return to his post. But more often he will fly down to the ground where his sharp eyes, even at a considerable distance, have seen a bee or a beetle alight. If he is hungry he will devour his prey at once, but if he is not he will place it in his larder. This explains his preference in trees, for he makes sure of his victims by spitting them. If you watch him closely you may be able to find his treasury, and there you will see not only bees and beetles but also young birds impaled on the thorns.

On commons or in cornfields near the coast you will find the common or corn bunting. He is plentiful there and in a number of scattered localities farther inland, but rare elsewhere, but even in his favourite haunts he is easily overlooked because of the plainness of his simple brown plumage. But he has a remarkable song which he sings persistently throughout spring and summer and which cannot be missed by any one with ears to hear. In the books you will find it described as like the jangling of keys or the tinkling of broken glass. These, and especially the jangling of keys, may give you some idea of the second part of the song, but they overlook the first part which is very important. The whole song sounds to me like, *chip-chip-chip-cherry-errier-ay*. The first three syllables are uttered slowly and the remainder hurriedly, but there is a distinct accent on the fourth, sixth and last syllables.

Now, the presence of the meadow-pipit on commons and other open spaces brings there another and still more interesting bird, namely the cuckoo, for the meadow-pipit is one of the birds chosen by the hen cuckoo as foster parent for her young. The cuckoo makes no nest of her own, but like other birds, the cock occupies a territory which he is prepared to defend against all comers of his own species. In order to demonstrate his right to his estate, he selects a prominent perch at various points on the extreme limits of it, and in the intervals of feeding and sleeping he visits these outposts and shouts from them his well-known call. This he does partly to warn his rivals that he is on the alert, but still more to attract the attention of any hen cuckoo that may happen to be in the neighbourhood. For this reason it is easy to attract him with even an indifferent imitation of his call, and you will find it worth your while to try the experiment. You must first, however, occupy a good hiding-place, not behind a trunk, for there you may have to show yourself if you wish to watch him, but under a screen of drooping branches where you may see without being seen.

In this way I have brought a cuckoo to within ten feet of me, and talked to him in his own tongue long enough to make some discoveries about him. He sat facing me and on a level with my eyes, so I was able to watch his every movement. The first thing I noticed was that he makes the two sounds in opposite ways, the first by drawing in air and the second by suddenly expelling it. While he is doing this a ball of air about the size of a pigeon's egg moves down and up in his neck. Then to my great surprise, I saw that he was calling without opening his bill, just as a pigeon coos. Pictures in books often show the cuckoo shouting with his mouth at full stretch.

Presently he did something that surprised me still more. He changed his call entirely. He kept to a double note, but said *zhee-zhee*, repeating it again and again. I have found that this is a call used by both cock and hen cuckoo at close quarters. The sound is something like the noise you make if you blow gently between the leaves of a book.

E.E.

E

If you attract a cuckoo he will most probably utter stil
another note when he arrives. It is quite unlike cuckoo, and
suggests rather a man coughing. It may be written down
thus, *wuh-cuh-cuh-cuh-cuh-cuh-cuh*. I think it is a note o
anger.

The hen cuckoo has a special call of her own. It sound
like water being poured quickly from a bottle. A good idea
of it can be given by pronouncing the word pup thus
pup-p-p-p-pup-pup-pup-pup-pup with the lips only and with
out exhaling breath. The object of this call is to tell the
cock that a hen is in his territory. If she were to use hi
note he might mistake her for a rival. But some observer
believe that the hen sometimes shouts cuckoo and that th
cocks occasionally use the bubble note. Proofs of this, how
ever, are still wanted, and you may perhaps find them.

The most conspicuous plant on the common is the gorse
whin, or furze as it is called in various parts of the country
There is an old saying that when the gorse is not in bloom
kissing is out of fashion. That just means that the gorse i
always in bloom. It does not, however, tell you the whol
truth, which is that there are two kinds of gorse whic
blossom at different seasons, the larger from November t
June and the smaller from June to October. The forme
grows into a large bush which may be three or more fee
in height. Its flowers are partly enclosed by two oute
yellowish leaflets which are covered with coarse blackis
hairs, and their two side petals or wings are longer than th
boat-shaped casquet or keel between them and curve ove
its tip. Its larger spines are deeply grooved and point mor
or less upwards. The dwarf species is smaller but may b
two or three feet high. Its flowers are smaller and paler, an
their wings are just about the same length as the keel, whil
their two outer leaflets are not so hairy as those of the large

species. Its main spines also are not more than $1\frac{1}{2}$ inches in length, and they curve backwards or downwards and are only very slightly grooved.

As you may guess from the form of its flower, the gorse belongs to the pea family. Consequently it grows its seeds in pods. These when ripe explode and scatter their contents. But the typical leaf of the pea family is not a hard, sharp spine, but a trefoil. Very early in its career the gorse shows its relationship in this way also. Its first leaves, after its two seedling leaves, are flat, soft trefoils.

A still smaller member of the pea family is the petty whin which has both spines and leafy branches.

The broom, another cousin, is a large shrub which grows as high as the common gorse but has small trefoil leaves and no spines. It makes a splendid show of yellow blossom in May. You will find it worth while on a sunny day to spend fifteen minutes beside a broom bush in full bloom and watch the coming and going of the bees, for you will then have a practical demonstration of the services rendered by the insects to the plants in return for honey. When the bee alights she places her forefeet on the wing-petals and her others on the sides of the keel, and by so doing she forces open the casquet so that she may thrust in her tongue and suck the sweet juices. But at the same time she releases the flowers which have been held on the stretch within the tip, and they shooting out like a spring, scatter pollen on her back. When this happens you should observe closely the seed-making flower. It is longer than the others and does not have a yellow top. Gradually it bends over till it is in such a position that, when another bee arrives, it touches her back and so is fertilised by pollen which she has brought from another blossom.

The little bird's-foot trefoil which blossoms among the

grass on the common belongs to the same family, but has quite a different method of utilising the bee. There is a tiny hole in the tip of her keel, and through this, when the weight of the bee depresses the casquet, the pollen is forced so that it clings to the underpart of her body, and later the seed-making flower protrudes through the same aparture and receives pollen from another bee.

A charming companion of the bird's-foot trefoil on the common is the tormentil. This little plant, though it has a bright yellow flower, belongs to the rose family. But whereas the rose and most of its relatives have five petals, this one has only four. Its leaves are stalkless, and are divided into three or five parts.

Where the grass is short and the ground dry you are sure to find two other tiny but very attractive flowers of the common, namely, eyebright and wild thyme. As they both grow in patches, they are quite conspicuous in spite of diminutive size. Eyebright is white or sometimes lilac striped with purple and has a bright yellow spot, which is probably the origin of the name, on what might be called its tongue. You should note this spot, for it is an invitation as much as to say, "Honey-seeking bees please alight here."

Thyme very frequently grows on little mounds which were once molehills. Its flowers are reddish purple, and they grow in circles at the top of the stalk, several of these whorls being packed close together so as to form a bunch

Eyebright is partly a parasite. Some of its rootlets penetrate the roots of grasses and draw nourishment from them. You will notice, however, that the plant has green leaves. That is a sure sign that it is able to do something for its own living.

Twining round the branches of gorse bushes, however you will often find a very strange plant which is a complet parasite. It has no leaves, but consists of long, red, thread-like stems which sometimes envelop the whole bush in an untidy tangle, and bear here and there little white flowers. This plant, which is called the dodder, begins its life in the ground where the seed produces a root and a stem. But as soon as the stem finds a living branch round which to twine, it drives suckers through the bark. The root then dies and the plant lives entirely on its host.

Down among the grass again you will find another remarkable little plant which has blue, pink, or white flowers. This is the milkwort. At first sight it seems to have only two petals. These, however, are not true petals, but are part of the green flower bracket, that is to say, they are sepals. Separate them and you will see the real petals within. They are much smaller, and by themselves would be of little service to the plant as an attraction to insects. The two side sepals have apparently been enlarged and coloured to make good their deficiency. But their colouring is only temporary. When the flower has been fertilised, they lie down and become ordinary green leaflets again.

Our two commonest thistles are also plentiful on this type of land, namely the spear thistle and the field thistle. The spear thistle is a tall plant, with leaves which may be a foot or more in length, all ending in a long lance-like point which is armed with a sharp spine, and with their blades broken up on both sides into a number of similar points. It bears only a few flower-heads and these are large with handsome plumed tops. We think of these heads as single flowers, but in reality they are made up of a large number of tiny florets each of which is a long tube with a five-pointed brim.

The field thistle is also known as the creeping thistle because its roots creep underground and send up many stems, each of which seems to be a plant in itself. You will notice that on some plants the flower-heads are more conspicuous than on others. These are the pollen flowers which in this species are always grown separately from the seedling flowers. Closer examination shows that the hard, green, prickly brackets of the former are almost round, whereas those of the latter are longer and show very little of the pink florets. The flower-heads are small and there are many on each plant, and the leaves, though very prickly, are not nearly so large or so fearsome as those of the spear thistle.

When the seeds are ripe the bracket expands and sets them free, and they float away each supported by a ring of long down, the separate hairs of which are given the greatest possible carrying power by being closely feathered.

The commons in summer swarm with insect life of many kinds. The most conspicuous are the butterflies. On a sunny day you will disturb at almost every step, a small heath butterfly or a common blue or a grayling. The small heath has light brown wings with dark margins and a dark spot in the top corner of each forewing. The female of the common blue butterfly is darkish brown with orange and black spots on the margins of her wings. The grayling is a larger butterfly about the size of the white butterfly which every one knows, and it is not grey but brown with a broad band of a lighter shade near the margins of both wings, and two dark spots in the band on each forewing.

In flight these butterflies are very conspicuous, but when they alight they disappear as if by magic. This is partly due to the way in which they fold their wings over the back, thus presenting only a thin line to the observer from one point of view, and also to the colouring on the underside of the wings which is a natural camouflage. The folding of the wings over the back like the closing of a book is the simplest means of distinguishing butterfly from moth; the moth folds its wings like a fan.

In consequence of their abundant insect life the commons are a happy hunting ground of spiders. Everywhere on the gorse or hawthorn bushes or among the long grass you will see the webs of many species. The orb nets of the garden spider and her cousins are as plentiful here as elsewhere, but the remarkable snare of the labyrinth spider is one of the most striking features of the common. It consists of a broad sheet of closely woven white silk with a round hole about the size of a penny in the middle of it. This hole is the entrance to a tube about an inch or more deep which is the den of the spider. Hidden within it she sits patiently waiting till some insect alights on the white sheet of her snare, and then in a moment she dashes out and pounces on it.

In August this spider makes a very wonderful nest at a little distance from her snare. It consists of a large outer shell, somewhat egg-like in form and with an entrance and an exit. That is all the average observer ever sees of it. But inside, and supported upright about the centre of the structure, is a cylindrical chamber, in which the cocoons are placed, and on each side between this and the outer wall are a number of passages running from front to back. This inner room is very seldom seen, because the nest as a rule is constructed during the night. If you are lucky enough to come upon one before it has been covered by the outer shell, you will agree with me that it is a marvellous work of art.

A little cousin of the labyrinth spider, which is also to be found on commons, makes an earthenware globe to cover its cocoon. You may find this attached to the side of a rush or to a branch of heather. It is beautifully rounded both inside and out and is strengthened with a mixture of silk.

In spring and early summer on open parts of the common where the ground is dry, you may come upon a snake basking in the sun. It may be lying on the short grass of a path, but if there is an old stump of a tree or a large stone, it will be coiled up on the top of that. Now more than ever is the time for the greatest caution, not because the creature will bite you, but because it will take alarm at the slightest sound and will wriggle away and vanish among the long grass. The adder is the only poisonous wild snake in England, but it does not make a practice of biting human beings. It is much more afraid of you than you are of it, and it will not bite you unless you molest it.

A full grown male adder which has just changed his skin is a very handsome fellow. He is easily recognised by his colours, which are white or yellowish with bold black zig-zag markings along his back beginning with a large V on his head. Unfortunately, however, his colours are not always so distinct. Just before sloughing they are much duller, and there is a dark variety of adder whose markings are hardly noticeable. It is possible to confuse him with harmless snakes, so when there is any doubt it behoves one to be very careful in approaching one of these reptiles.

The adder is from eighteen inches to two feet in length. The grass snake, which is harmless, is a yard or more in length when full grown. But the grass snake prefers damp situations and long grass, and may be recognised at once by its conspicuous collar of white or yellow.

Another reptile which is often by beginners mistaken for the adder is the slow-worm, which is not a snake at all but a lizard. Now lizards as a rule have four legs, but the slow-worm has none. Underneath its skin, however, the rudiments of legs have been found, and so its relationship to the lizards has been established.

The slow-worm is so called because, unlike the snakes, it is slow to take alarm. If you find one sunning itself, you will be able to go right up to it and even touch it before it will become aware of its danger. On short grass or bare ground its movements are not rapid, but when it reaches long grass it disappears as quickly as any snake. The slow-worm has a smooth, polished skin of a silvery or copper shade.

You may also find two species of four-footed lizard. They are fascinating little creatures, and it is delightful to watch them darting about when they are hunting for insects. The common lizard is brown with dark bands running from head to tail. It lives in more or less damp situations. The sand lizard, as its name implies, prefers dry sandy banks.

CHAPTER FIVE

STREAMS

On the banks of any slow-flowing stream on any day in th
year you may come upon the water-rat. He is one of ou
very few day-loving quadrupeds, and he is such a charmin
little fellow and so inoffensive that it is a great pity he ha
been given such an unfortunate name. He is not a rat, bu
be belongs to the family that includes the rat, so the nam
would serve quite well but for the fact that the commo
brown rat, which is so destructive and undesirable, invade
his domain in summer, and burrows in the banks and swim
in the stream, much as he does. The consequence of this i
that the two animals are constantly confused, and th
innocent one lives under the shadow of the other's evil re
putation and frequently suffers martyrdom. I wish ever
one who reads this to learn to distinguish the two, and s
help to save the true water-rat from this gross injustic

For this purpose it is necessary to call him by his other name, which is less well-known but fits him much better. He belongs to the same section of the family as the field vole and the bank vole, so he is really the water vole. He has a fine coat of long, thick brown fur, and has a short, broad head with a rounded nose, and small ears which are hidden among the hair. By these points you will easily recognise him. The rat is a larger animal with a long, narrow, protruding snout and prominent ears. At close quarters you will notice that the water vole's tail is covered with long hairs whereas the rat's tail is scaly.

If you are noisy in your progress along the bank you will disturb the water vole, and he will announce his presence by diving into the water with a loud plunge. If you are quick you may see him darting away under water, paddling only with his strong hind legs, or swimming on the surface close to the bank with only head and shoulders showing. Then if he vanishes you may know that he has sought refuge in his burrow, the front entrance of which is under water. But if you sit down and wait, he will presently appear again and you may watch him feeding.

He will dive and, swimming under water, will select the juicy stem of some plant that appeals to his fancy. This he will bite off and carry back to the bank, where he will sit up on his haunches and nibble it. Then he will dive for another and so on. You will notice that when he emerges his fur is quite dry. He is a vegetarian, but he does not confine himself entirely to water plants. He will often make an excursion into an adjoining wood or garden, but it is not so easy to watch his doings there as on the river bank.

Another very attractive animal of the sluggish stream is the water shrew. He is similar in form to the common shrew but larger, and his colour is black above and white underneath. He dives and swims under water for his food which consists of insects and their larvæ, snails, small fish and frog spawn. It is fascinating to watch him while he is at work, but still more so while he is at play, for he is delightfully gay and frolicsome and so forms a charming contrast to the very sedate water vole. When they are not feeding, two or three water shrews will chase each other playfully up and down the pool, now under water, now skipping along the surface, now running up or down the reeds or paying a brief visit to the bank and then plunging again. In the course of these gambols one of the party may jump right out of the water.

One peculiarity of the water shrew is that when it is swimming on the surface the whole of its head and back are visible, its nose being held high in the air.

The king of our four-footed water animals is the otter. He is our largest member of the weasel tribe and measures three feet six inches including his tail, which is long, thick and strong. By nature he is a lover of sunlight, and may sometimes be seen abroad by day, but he has been so much persecuted on account of his destruction of fish that he has taken to hunting and playing by night.

Many birds that are common elsewhere are to be seen among the trees and bushes on the banks of our streams, but there are several species that find their living either in or near running water and they should always be looked for there. Chief among them is the kingfisher, whose brilliant blue back and red breast are a wonder and a delight to behold. Apart from his colouring you may recognise him by his heavy head, with its long, strong, sharp bill and by his short tail. He frequently visits ponds and ditches and, in winter, even the sea, but his favourite haunt is a sluggish

The king of our four-footed water animals is the otter.

stream. If a blue streak flashes past you right in the middle and close to the water, you may know that it is the kingfisher. But to see him at his best you must watch him at work.

Where there are overhanging bushes or posts standing up out of the water he perches at feeding time and watches the stream flowing beneath him. Then suddenly he flies down swiftly, plunges into the water and returns to his seat with some prey in his mouth. If it is a fish, he kills it by beating it several times on his perch, and then he turns it in his bill and swallows it head first.

Where, however, there is no suitable perch he is still able to fish, for if in his passage up or down stream he spies some possible prey, he pauses and hovers over it for some moments till it comes close enough to the surface, and then he plunges. I have seen him do this at various heights from three or four up to ten or twelve feet above the water.

On fast-flowing rocky streams the kingfisher is unknown, but his place is taken by the equally interesting dipper.

This little bird is a distant cousin of the common wren, and when you see him you will notice the family likeness in his form. But he is easily recognised by the fact that his plumage is all black, or apparently so, except his breast which is white. He runs about briskly on the rocky margins of the stream, or sits on a stone with his feet quite still but his body constantly bobbing up and down. It is from this peculiar habit that he has been given his name, though it happens to apply equally well to his very remarkable method of feeding.

There is nothing in his appearance to suggest that he is anything but an ordinary perching bird like the wren. His feet are the feet of a percher and are not in any way suited

or swimming, yet he obtains his food from the bottom of
he stream. He enters the water sometimes by plunging
rom a stone, but more frequently he walks in deliberately
ill it is deep enough for swimming and then he disappears.
t used to be thought that he was able to walk on the bed
of the stream in spite of the buoyancy of the water, but if
you can watch him at work from an overhanging bank you
will see that he actually swims. He swims, however, in a
way of his own. He does not use his feet as other water
birds do, but paddles along with his wings.

The grey wagtail is another bird of the fast-flowing
streams, so he may be seen, most commonly, in hilly
districts. But he may be found also on sluggish lowland
rivers by those who know where to look for him. For some
reason or other he is particularly fond of waterfalls, and
frequently nests by the side of one. So even in the most
unlikely country it is worth while looking out for him
whenever you come upon a waterfall.

There is much yellow in his plumage, so it is necessary
to be able to distinguish him from his cousin the yellow
wagtail. Both birds have bright yellow underparts, but in
summer the grey wagtail's throat is black spotted with
white. The grey wagtail is blue-grey above, and the yellow
wagtail light olive green with a bright yellow mark over
the eye. The yellow wagtail, however, is not a bird of the
streams, but favours the open meadows, and is only a
summer visitor.

On the banks of streams or ponds or on marshy ground
in summer you are certain to meet with the sedge warbler.
He is different from most other birds in this respect that,
instead of flying away from you, he will come out of hiding
and sing at you in a very excited way. I think that in this
he shows real courage, and that his intention is not to show

off but to attract your attention to himself so that you will not trouble to look for the nest. It is impossible to describe his song because it is so varied, but when you know it you will discover that he often mixes in with it scraps which he has imitated from the songs of other birds. You will have no difficulty in recognising him, for he is a little brown bird with a white breast and a bold buff streak above his eye. His brown back and head are streaked with darker brown, but the feature to look for specially is the eye stripe.

On sluggish streams two other wonderful winged creatures will delight you with their beauty. They are the demoiselle dragonflies. Most dragonflies prefer ponds or ditches, but the two species of demoiselle confine themselves to streams, and curiously enough they are usually found on different streams or on different parts of the same stream and very seldom together. Unlike our other species of dragonfly, their wings are beautifully coloured and graceful in form, and their manner of flight is feeble and uncertain like that of a butterfly. One of them has its wings almost entirely tinted with the same rich blue as its body, and the other has a large patch of blue on each wing towards the tip. The former you will find where the stream is shaded with overhanging bushes, and the latter where the banks are covered only with rank herbage.

By the character of their flight you might think that they were mild and inoffensive in disposition, but if you watch them you will find that they are fierce and carnivorous like their cousins of the pond, though they have not the same strong, swift, piratical kind of action. They sit on bush or herbage with their wings folded over their backs, and in this position they are almost invisible. But if a caddis-fly flutters near them they dash out and seize it, then alight again and devour it wings and all.

The caddis-fly is easily mistaken for a moth, but its wings are covered with short hairs instead of with scales. Its early life, however, is the most interesting part of its career. This it spends in the water, and as it is a naked, vegetable-feeding grub, with no weapons with which to defend itself against its enemies, it builds a house in which it lives and which it carries about wherever it goes.

This case of the caddis-worm is a very wonderful structure. It varies in form and material according to the species that makes it. For example, in sluggish water where water-weed grows and consequently molluscs abound, it may consist entirely of snail shells, or of leaf stalks, or pieces of stick cut to suitable lengths and bound together with silk. Some species, however, prefer a sandy bottom. They build their cases of grains of sand, and you will notice that they are careful to select grains of a size. Others prefer a gravelly bed, and build their homes of tiny pebbles, and so on.

The mayfly is another insect of sluggish streams and ponds, but it is to be seen on only three or four days in the year, about the end of May or the beginning of June. When it does appear it comes in such huge numbers that you cannot miss it if you are by the stream side, and it is quite easily identified. It has four wings, but the hind pair are very small. You may know it, however, before you have time to inspect its wings, by the fact that it has several bristles about the length of its body sticking straight out from the tip of its tail.

The marvel of the mayfly's life is that it becomes a winged insect at all. Like the caddis-worm it spends most of its existence under water, and acquires wings for only a few hours of glorious freedom in the air. Even then it has so many enemies and is so voraciously preyed upon by them

that only a few individuals enjoy that brief freedom t
the full.

Its career as an adult being so short, it has no need fo
food, and consequently its mouth parts are not full
developed. But in one respect it is quite unique amon;
insects. All other species, when they emerge from the pup
and launch themselves into the air on their first fligh
have reached the final stage of their development. Not s
the mayfly. It has still another change to make. Its firs
flight is short, no farther than from the empty pupa cas
floating on the surface of the stream to some overhangin
branch. There it alights and remains for a time. Presentl
its skin, which is of a greenish hue, splits and the adul
emerges, wings and all, and sets forth in search of a mat
leaving behind an empty shell of a completely winge
insect.

Among the trees and bushes on the banks of the strear
you will find most of those that are to be seen elsewher
but there are two which can only flourish there or in oth
damp situations, namely, the willow and the alder. In ear
spring you may easily recognise the alder by the fact the
it produces rusty brown lamb's-tail catkins. In summer i
leaves are quite distinctive. They are heart-shaped, but th
notch of the heart is where you would expect to find the t
of the leaf. They look as if by some strange accident the
had been grown the wrong way round. In winter it ha
four features which are worthy of notice. Its leaf buds a
grown each on a little stalk of its own. In this the alder
unique among our British trees. Besides these it has tw
kinds of flower bud. Those of the lamb's-tail catkins a
long and sausage-shaped. The seed-making buds are sma
and resemble the leaf buds in size and form, but differ fro
them in the fact that they are usually grown in litt

bunches whereas the leaf buds are always single. The fruits are somewhat like small pine cones. Some may be empty, and in that case their scales will be wide open, but others may not shed their seeds till spring.

The willow which you may know by its long, narrow, pale green leaves, provides its seeds with downy parachutes by means of which the wind scatters them far and wide. Enormous quantities of them, however, must be wasted through being blown on to unsuitable ground. The seeds of the alder simply drop into the water, but they are so constructed that they float, and so they are carried down stream until they are cast on some part of the bank where they can start life on their own account.

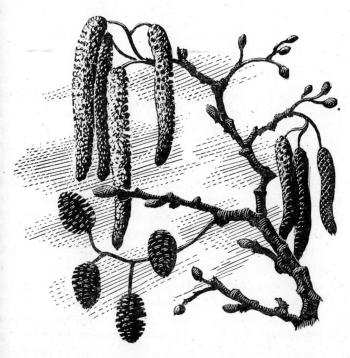

CHAPTER SIX

PONDS

WATER VOLE, water shrew and otter may be seen on ponds
and lakes as well as on streams, and so may the kingfisher.
On the other hand the water hen may be seen on streams
as well as on ponds. This is the commonest of all our
water birds. He is more usually called the moorhen. That
name is misleading, for the bird is not confined to moors
and, indeed, must be very rarely seen on them. But it is
probably a corruption of merehen, which is a fair description of the species, for wherever there is a shallow pond,
however small, there also you are sure to find the water
hen. If you do not see him you will hear his call, which is
a harsh croak sounding like *kur-r-ruck*.

When you see him he may be either stepping about
calmly in a field adjoining the bank or swimming about
among the water weeds. You may recognise him by his

black plumage and bobbing tail which is white underneath, and also by a bright red patch on his forehead. When he sees you he will make for the bank, and will hide there till he thinks you are gone.

His cousin, the coot, is a somewhat larger bird. He is also black, but is easily distinguished by a conspicuous white patch on his forehead. The coot is more purely a water bird than the water hen. He avoids the banks and very seldom comes ashore except when the pond is frozen. When he is alarmed he either takes refuge among the reeds or contents himself with swimming towards the farther shore. Nevertheless, he is a vegetarian. His food consists of water weed which he obtains by diving.

The ordinary call note of the coot sounds to me like *coit* repeated several times, so the name coot may be a corruption of this. But he has others besides this, one of which, an expression of anger, is remarkably like the noise made by the pulling of a cork.

Another relative of the water hen is the water rail. This bird is not uncommon but he is very seldom seen because his habit is to feed on the mud among the reeds, and though he can both fly and swim well he spends his days there unless he is disturbed. When the pond is reduced by drought or other causes so that an area of mud is left between the water and the reeds, he frequently ventures out from his cover, and then he may be watched feeding. He is well worth seeing if only on account of his remarkable colouring.

The little grebe, or dabchick, is easily confused with the water hen by beginners on account of his size, though really he is several inches shorter than that bird. He is a brownish black bird with chestnut on throat and neck, and with almost no tail. He prefers the smaller ponds and dives for his living.

When he is alarmed he dives, swims several yards under water, comes up for a moment and dives again, repeating the manœuvre till he is well out of danger. Or he dives and remains submerged, and like a submarine, can lie just under the surface for a considerable time with only his bill protruding to obtain air. Presently he pops up his head to reconnoitre, and if he is not satisfied he sinks again, but if he thinks you have passed on, his neck and body will gradually appear and he will go on with his ordinary pursuits. His spring call is very remarkable. It is like the whinnying of a horse.

On lakes and reservoirs you will see the great crested grebe, a large bird with a long neck and a sharp bill, whose general colouring is black above and white underneath. In summer he has a black double crest which is suggestive of upright ears, and a chestnut and black ruff, or "tippett" as it is called, round the lower part of the head.

He is a wonderful diver and swimmer, and as he preys upon fish which he pursues under water, he never comes up where he goes down. Sometimes, when he is swimming near the surface or in shallow water, you may follow his course by a ripple, which his passage creates, but as a rule he appears in most unexpected quarters, and may even have come up and gone down more than once before you spy him again. He spends most of his time in the water, seldom if ever comes ashore, and does not fly until in autumn he migrates to the sea.

Ducks on the other hand often pass hours on the banks, sleeping or preening, and frequently take long flights except during a few weeks in late summer when they are moulting. When they return to the lake after one of these journeys they plane down gradually and, as they near the surface, drop their feet and hind part of the body and glide along

Ducks often pass hours on the banks, sleeping or preening.

thus for a yard or so with a swish of divided water till their momentum is exhausted.

Various species of duck either dwell in or visit our ponds and lakes. The common wild duck or mallard is easily recognised by his brilliant blue-green head and neck and white collar and also by his curly tail. The shoveller duck also has a green head but his neck is white. His most conspicuous feature, however, is his broad shovel-like bill which gives him an ungainly appearance. A broad band of chestnut on his breast will also help you to identify him. The teal is much smaller than the mallard, but unless the two birds are close enough for comparison, size is not a reliable guide. The clearest and simplest identity mark of the teal is a light brown patch on the side near the tail.

These three species are surface-feeding ducks. They feed after the manner of the common domestic duck, that is by plunging the head under water, tipping up the body, if necessary, so that they seem to be standing on their heads, and searching the mud at the bottom with the broad flat beak for anything animal or vegetable that may appeal to them. In ordinary circumstances they never dive.

The tufted duck and the pochard, which are also common species, obtain their food by diving. The tufted duck is black, with a large white patch on his side. His tuft is a streamer of long feathers that hangs over the back of his head. The pochard has a red head and neck and a silvery back.

Often in winter you may see mixed companies of duck at some distance from the shore and may have difficulty in distinguishing their colours. There are certain well marked features, however, by which you may easily pick out the diving ducks from the surface-feeders, and that is an important step towards identification. The surface-feeding ducks all carry their tails well in the air, whereas the diving ducks swim low in the water with their tails trailing like the stern of a motor boat. Again, the diving ducks as a rule carry their heads tucked well down between the shoulders, and this gives them a characteristic pose which you will soon learn to recognise at a glance. When they take to flight they have some difficulty in starting, and flap along the surface for a yard or two before they are able to rise. On the other hand, the surface-feeding ducks can fly up almost perpendicularly from the water. In flight the two can be distinguished by the shape of the wings, those of the divers being short and somewhat rounded and those of the surface-feeders longer and more pointed.

In winter a number of other species of duck visit our ponds and lakes. The widgeon has a chestnut head with a buff forehead, and the drake announces his presence by a peculiar whistling call which sounds like *peel*. The pintail, as his name implies, has a long, sharp tail, somewhat like a pheasant's. A large duck that holds his tail well in the air and has a conspicuous white patch on his wing is the gadwall, and a small one about the size of the teal with a bold white stripe over his eye is the garganey. The goldeneye is a small diving duck with a large white patch on his cheek. Other interesting strangers are the three fish-eating ducks, goosander, red-breasted merganser, and smew. These birds have long necks and narrow tapering bills and, being divers, swim low in the water. There is no difficulty in identifying the smew by his plumage, which at a distance seems to be pure white but is really pied, with two black patches on the head and a black back. The goosander has a dark green crested head, a black back, and white breast and wings, and the red-breasted merganser is similar, but has red on the breast and the lower part of the neck, which gives him a distinct white collar, and also a black and white checked band on his shoulder.

All these birds have frequently been seen even on London lakes and reservoirs by people whose eyes are keen enough to notice such interesting strangers, and who have the enterprise to visit such spots to look for them.

On the banks you may see the sedge warbler which I have described in the chapter on "Streams," but wherever there is a bed of reeds you should look specially for his cousin, the reed warbler. This little bird seldom leaves the shelter of the reed beds, and even there he is so restless that it is often very difficult to get a good view of him. But when you do see him you will know him by the fact that he does not have a conspicuous buff stripe above his eye. His plumage is plain brown above and white underneath, whereas the sedge warbler has dark markings on his head and back and the eye-stripe.

If you throw a few pieces of gravel into a bed of reeds which you believe to be the home of a reed warbler, he will at once start singing if he is there. His song is a jerky performance, a few simple phrases repeated again and again. One very distinctive phrase is *chirra-chirra*. The song is not so loud or so varied as that of the sedge warbler. The latter bird, on the other hand, is much more excited and explosive than the reed warbler and often utters some very harsh notes. Nevertheless, even experienced observers have some times difficulty in distinguishing the two songs apart.

Another common bird of the pond bank is the reed bunting. He is a cousin of the yellow hammer which is so familiar on the hedgerows, and he is easily identified by his velvety black head and throat and white collar which make him very conspicuous. His back is reddish brown with darker markings, and he is about the size of a sparrow. He

This little bird, the reed warbler, seldom leaves the shelter of the reed beds.

has a very simple song which he sings constantly from the top of a bush. It sounds like *chip-chip-cherry*, but sometimes he adds two or three more notes. The first one I knew sang regularly seven notes and varied the song occasionally with nine.

Flitting about, fairylike, near the surface of the pond or among the bushes or over the herbage on the bank you will see several species of dragonfly, their slender, graceful bodies coloured bright blue and black, red and black or yellow and black. They are sun-loving creatures, and if a passing cloud obscures the sunlight for a little they disappear immediately. But if you examine the bushes and herbage you will find them clinging there with their wings folded over their backs. It is this closing of the wings that accounts for their seemingly miraculous disappearance.

Several much larger species of dragonfly are also common, though they are never to be seen in such numbers as these graceful little sylphs. They are fierce piratical fellows, and dash swiftly hither and thither in pursuit of their insect prey or of each other, but when they alight most of them hold their wings outstretched.

There are over forty species of dragonfly in this country, but it is astonishing how little is known about them. They offer a splendid field for any young naturalist who wishes to do original work.

They spend most of their lives under water in the form of very ugly grubs. If you examine the reeds or rushes growing out of the water you may find some of the empty skins from which the wonderful winged dragonflies have emerged. These are nymph skins, the third stage in the creature's life corresponding to the chrysalis stage of the butterfly, but they give a good idea of the ugliness of the insect before it appears in its resplendent perfection. That part of the dragonfly's life has been carefully studied and photographed in aquaria. The part that is not so well known is how the females dispose of their eggs, and that can only be satisfactorily ascertained by close observation of the creatures in their natural haunts. Each species seems to have a method of its own.

The dragonfly practises marriage by capture. With the tip of his tail he seizes his wife by the back of her neck, and thus they fly about together for some time. It is common to see the small blue species mated. If you watch them you will see them settle on a floating leaf, and while the female rests there at full length the male stands upright on her neck like an acrobat. Then the female will move her tail about restlessly. At each change she pierces the skin of the leaf and deposits an egg underneath it. When the leaf dies it will sink to the bottom and the eggs will hatch there.

Some species alight on the surface of the water and deposit their eggs there. This must be a hazardous start for the new generation, for the water is full of hungry creatures ready to snap up such tit-bits as they sink. One large species, which I call Aladdin because the broad, thick body of the male is encrusted with a coat of wonderful pale blue gems, takes this risk also, but acts in a different manner. The female is not blue but dull orange in colour. She hovers over the water and smacks her tail down into it repeatedly, depositing an egg at each dip. This and other large species do not remain in pairs during the egg-laying process. Another large species, which I call the Mandarin, seems to sow its eggs at random on the water also, but its actual method of doing so has not been described. It has a longer and thinner body than Aladdin and is coloured black and yellow.

Still another common monster has a variegated colouring, consisting of brown profusely marked with black, yellow, green and blue. My name for it is the Pirate. I have watched it laying eggs, and its method is very interesting. It alights on a plant that is growing out of the pond, and dipping its tail into the water, pierces the stalk an inch or so below the surface and deposits the eggs there. So they are under water and in a place of safety from the beginning. You may frequently see both the Mandarin and the Pirate hawking hither and thither at a considerable distance from water.

I have given the name Jolly Roger to a large brown dragonfly which I have frequently seen flying over or near pools in pine woods. There is a black three-cornered patch on each hindwing which suggests the notorious flag.

The dragonfly breathes, as other insects do, through what are known as spiracles, which are tiny round openings like portholes placed at intervals along each side of its body. But the dragonfly larva breathes by inhaling and exhaling water through its tail.

Other pond creatures have different methods of breathing. If you watch them you will see that some come to the surface for a moment or two every now and again. The water beetle thrusts the tip of his tail above the surface and takes in a supply of air under his wing cases, and then is able to swim down into the depths again and remain there for some time. He is the true forerunner of the submarine of the future which, besides swimming under water, will be able to run on land and fly through the air, for he can do all three things.

The water spider also requires to visit the surface for air, but she deals with it in another way. She collects it round her body by means of her hairy coat and then swims down looking like a silvery globe. Her progress is slow because the air tends to drag her upwards, but at length she manages to reach a point among the water weed where she comes to rest. There she has woven herself a silken tent. Into this she releases the air and then returns to the surface for more, and so on till she has filled her den with it, and so can live and breathe there like a man in a diving bell till the supply is exhausted.

The tadpoles of frogs, toads and newts breathe at first by sucking in water by the mouth and expelling it through gills after the manner of fish. But as they grow up and their legs and heads begin to appear they also develop lungs to enable them to breathe air when at length they are old enough to leave the water. When this happens they pay frequent visits to the surface, and you may see them there with their mouths protruding. In time the gills disappear altogether, and the fully developed but not full grown, animals are able to come out on dry land.

The eggs of frogs and toads are similar, but those of the frog are laid in masses and those of the toad in long strings. The newt lays her eggs singly and deposits each on a separate leaf. As she does so she doubles up the leaf to protect the treasure.

The tadpoles of frogs and toad are also very much alike, and they pass through a similar series of changes, the hind legs appearing first, then the fore legs, and then the tail becoming absorbed. The tadpoles of the newt, however, differ in this respect, that their fore legs appear before their hind legs and that they retain their tails.

The toad has a dark, dry warty skin and spends all its adult life on land except for a short time in spring when the eggs are laid. The frog is lighter in colour and his skin is smooth and moist. He hops about a great deal on land, but he prefers damp ground and is never far from a pond, or a

pool or a ditch into which he can plunge when he feels
inclined. Young newts, on the other hand, after they come
ashore for the first trip do not return to the water till they
are three or four years old, by which time they are full
grown. Meanwhile they spend their days in hiding and
come out to feed at night. So at this stage of their career
they are very seldom seen. Every spring, however, many
adult newts find their way to the ponds, and there you may
easily watch them swimming about and feeding. You will
notice that they do not swim with their legs as frogs do
but by means of the tail.

There are three species of newt in this country, two of
which, the common or smooth newt and the great warty
newt, are quite common. The former is about four and the
latter about six inches in length. The warty newt is almost
black above and bright orange underneath, and the smooth
newt is lighter above and marked all over with conspicuous
dark spots. The males have large saw-like crests on their
backs and tails.

On small stagnant ponds and ditches the surface often in
the course of the summer becomes covered with a coat of
green. This is duckweed, and consists of a vast number of
tiny separate plants each comprising two or more small
leaflets or "fronds," as they are called and a number of
little rootlets which dangle from them like the stinging
rays of a jelly fish. But though these hanging parts are
called rootlets they are not attached to anything. The
plants are free, and are capable of being moved from side
to side of the pond by wind or other force without coming
to any harm.

At the end of the summer the duckweed disappears, but
next spring it appears again as if by magic. The plant sometimes produces flowers and seeds, but these are so minute

that they are hardly ever noticed. What happens as a rule, however, is that at the approach of winter the plant stores up its life and a sufficiency of food in a tiny bulb. This sinks to the bottom and lies there till spring, when it rises to the surface again and opens out new fronds to the sun. Duckweed multiplies partly by seed, but mostly by throwing off parts of itself which become new plants.

Another very interesting plant of our ponds is the water buttercup. Except that their petals are white, its flowers are like those of the common buttercup. But it has two kinds of leaves. Those which appear above the surface are broad and broken up into three rounded leaflets or lobes. Those that grow under water are quite different. They consist of a bunch of threads. For this remarkable difference there must be a good explanation. It is believed that these threads enable the plant to obtain carbonic acid from the water more readily than the broad upper leaves could, for the water is on all sides of each thread whereas it could pass over two sides only of a flat leaf. The necessity for the difference lies in the fact that there is less carbonic acid in water than there is in air.

This plant varies very much according to the situation in which it grows. In deep ponds and in streams all the leaves may be submerged and they will then all be of the thread-like kind. You will notice a difference, however, between those in ponds and those in streams. The threads of the former are short and spread out in all directions like the rays of a star, whereas the threads of the latter are longer and lie more or less parallel to one another. There is another species which grows in shallow water or on mud at the side of a pond. It has smaller flowers and no thread-like leaves, whereas its broad leaves are angled rather than rounded, from which fact it is called the ivy-leaved buttercup.

E.E.

Other water plants besides the water buttercups have thread-like leaves. The water violet has no others, and only its flower stalk grows above the surface. In spite of it name this plant is not a violet but a cousin of the primrose The name refers to the colour of the petals which are a beautiful pale mauve. They are borne in several circle round the stalk.

Still another is the bladder-wort. This also has only submerged thread-like leaves. It has no roots but float freely in the water. You will notice on the leaves a number of tiny air balls. It is probable that, like the bladders on a fisherman's net and on the common seaweed called bladder wrack, these help to support the plant near the surface especially when it sends up its flower stalk which, with th large yellow blossoms, must tend to weigh it down. The are also, however, little traps. Each has an entrance with a tiny door which opens from the outside but not from th inside. Water fleas and other minute creatures often push their way in, and once they do that they cannot get out again. They soon die and their bodies are digested by th plant.

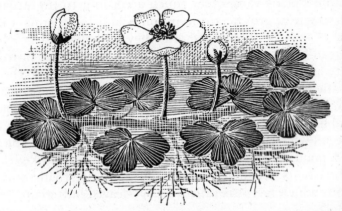

CHAPTER SEVEN

WAYSIDES AND WASTES

THE wonders that are to be found on any wayside or waste piece of ground would thrill the heart of any budding explorer. For example, you may discover there the nest of a wasp or a bee. Most of us are satisfied to think of the wasp simply as the wasp and to kill her at sight, but she may be one of several species, some of which nest underground and some in bushes.

When the summer is well advanced, you cannot help knowing where a colony of underground wasps are nesting any more than you could pass unnoticed the spot where miners have been labouring, because of the great tip of excavated material that has been thrown out of the workings. Wasps, like bees, are very fond of sweetness, but unlike bees they do not store it in the shape of honey. Most of their energies are devoted to building and digging. As

builders they require raw materials, but they do not use
wax as the bees do. Instead, they manufacture paper and
construct their homes of that. The raw material of the
paper is the same as that used so largely by human paper-
makers in the last half century, namely wood, and the
source from which it is obtained is decaying trees and old
fences and gates. The wasp has very powerful jaws which
enable it to tear minute strips from the more weather-worn
portions of exposed wood. You will hear it doing so if you
watch one at work. The sound it makes is like the scraping
of a mouse. The insect chews this material and so converts
it into a soft pulp, a little ball of which it carries off in its
legs to the nest.

But before the nest is begun, and afterwards day by day
as it increases in size, there is another very important fea-
of engineering that has to be accomplished by the wasps.
In spring the queen wasp takes possession of some existing
burrow, such as the deserted home of a bank vole, and her
first operation is to enlarge this so as to form a cave of
suitable shape and size to accommodate the top floor of her
dwelling. She digs the earth with her jaws and carries it
out of the burrow between her legs. As her family increases
new and larger floors have to be added to the nest, and to
make room for them the height and girth of the cave have
to be increased. Throughout the summer the two operations are carried on concurrently by the workers, and
consequently as the weeks advance, a quantity of earth
accumulates outside below the entrance. If you have the
courage to remain still close to the burrow and watch the
wasps coming and going, you will see that they enter
carrying supplies either of food or pulp, food most probably
in the shape of dismembered flies, and come away bearing
a load of earth or a small pebble. The pebbles being

heavy burden for such a tiny labourer, are dropped at once, but the earth is carried a little farther and probably much of it is borne right away. If your eyesight is not quick enough to see this happening, you can satisfy yourself that it does happen by examining the tip of excavated material. You will find that the pebbles and the larger grains of earth are lying nearest to the entrance.

The nests of the underground wasps are similar to those which are so commonly constructed in gooseberry and currant bushes or in other shrubs. They are hung up to the roof of the cave by a stout rope of paper, and consist of several papier-maché discs of various sizes, the smallest being at the top and the bottom and the largest in the middle, which are cleverly hung parallel to each other by means of two or more paper strings. These suspended floors are enclosed by a thin sheet of grey paper, which is attached to the main support and hangs closely round them and so gives the nest very much the appearance of a Chinese lantern, except that the opening is at the bottom instead of at the top.

The discs are flat and smooth above, but underneath they are covered with a large number of hexagonal cells in which the young wasps hang, during the first few weeks of their lives, head downwards.

It is a great pity that wasps have to be destroyed, because the greater part of the food on which they are reared consists of insects. In spring and early summer you may see a queen wasp searching the hedgerows for prey. It is not uncommon for a wasp to attack a spider in its web, and I have seen one, in a room where there was tempting jam on the table, pounce on a house fly, sting it, nip off its wings and limbs, and sail away with the carcase between its legs.

The bumble bees are also social insects and most of them

nest in the ground. There are several species of them in this country, and they are more easily distinguished from each other than wasps are, because of the various colours of their furry coats. The two commonest are the golden bar and the red tail. These names are my own, so you will not find them in the text books. Strange to tell, these beautiful, familiar, and interesting creatures have been so neglected by naturalists that, like the dragonflies, they have never been given any but scientific names. The golden bar is the common bumble bee, which is black with a yellow band at the neck and another across the middle of the abdomen and a white tail.

There are two or three other quite common species which are very like her, but by careful observation you will notice differences. One which I call the bramble bee, because she is very fond of bramble blossom, is almost exactly the same except that her tail is red. Another, which I have named the wedding ring, is yellow with a large black patch on the middle of the thorax which thus forms the ring, a broad black band across the middle of the abdomen and a white tail.

The red tail is all black except on the tail. This is not a good name, because there are other species of similar colouring to which it would apply equally well. One of these is common and may be distinguished from the red tail only by the facts that it has a shorter and therefore rounder abdomen, and has red hairs on its legs instead of black. I have not yet thought of a suitable name for this species, but another which has a complete coat of reddish yellow I have called teddy bear. The field bee has a reddish yellow thorax and a black abdomen with a double yellow band at the tail, and the wood or carder bee is yellow with a black patch on the thorax, a broad and a narrow black band across the middle of the abdomen and a red tail.

Some of my names may perhaps become popular, but, if by suggesting them I have succeeded in interesting you and others in these delightful insects, still better ones may be found. But what is more important, I shall have introduced you to a wide and little known branch of nature which is full of fascinating problems, which the energy and enterprise of young explorers may help to solve. For example, there is the astonishing fact that there are cuckoos among bees and wasps as well as among birds.

Besides the social species, there are hundreds of other bees and wasps which are solitary or live in colonies consisting of many separate nests. In spring you may often come upon little pyramids of freshly powdered earth. Worm casts are spiral and, being damp, form a solid mass, but these consist of light earth which has been excavated grain by grain, and you might think that they were the beginnings of mole hills. They are the work of a solitary bee. Underneath them is a mine which, when it is completed, will be from six inches to a foot in depth. At intervals in the sides of this shaft the bee digs little cells. In each of these she places a store of pollen on the top of which she deposits an egg, and when she has completed her task, she seals up the entrance to the shaft with earth. When the grubs hatch, each has enough food to serve it till it reaches the pupa stage of its existence in which it requires none. Then it lies dormant all winter and emerges as a perfect bee the following spring.

Other species nest in sandy banks, in branches of bramble, in rotten wood, in old snail shells and so on, and each has habits of its own.

Another attractive insect of the footpath is the tiger beetle. He is green, marked with several yellow spots, and unlike most other beetles he is very nimble and energetic. He has to be, because he lives by preying on other insects. He has efficient wings tucked away beneath his neat green wing cases, or elytra as they are called, but he prefers to do his hunting on the ground, for he is a swift runner. He is constantly on the move, and the moment an insect alights within reasonable reach of him, he charges at it with marvellous rapidity and very seldom fails to capture it.

This is very different from his method of securing prey while he is a grub. Then he has short legs suited only for crawling, so in order to secure his active insect prey he has to resort to stratagem. He digs a pit about two or three inches in depth in the bank close by, and clinging to one side near the top with his tail, and pressing his back, which is armed with two special hooks on a little hump, against the opposite side, he fills the entrance with his head and waits. Whenever an insect comes near enough, he seizes it with a very rapid movement of his head and at once drops to the bottom of his pit where he devours the victim at his leisure.

Compare this with the clumsy movements of the dumbledor beetle, which booms heavily across the road in the evening and most probably blunders into your face on the way. This is a large black beetle, and is a cousin of the scarab, the famous sacred beetle of Egypt. Like its relative it is a scavenger, making burrows in the ground where it lays its eggs in stores of dung on which its young will feed when they hatch.

The sexton beetle is also a scavenger but confines its attentions to carrion. If you leave the dead body of a mouse on an unfrequented path, you will probably before long have a chance to watch this interesting insect at work. Its method is to excavate the earth from underneath the dead animal, and so to lower it gradually into a grave and cover it up. But its aim is not to clear away an object that may be offensive to man, but to provide a plentiful supply of food for its young, so when it has completed the burial it lays its eggs in the corpse.

The beautiful fairy lights which we see among the herbage of the roadsides on summer evenings, are the signals of the glow-worm, which is really a beetle. If you examine the insect you will find that it is wingless and has a soft body like that of a caterpillar. You will notice also that it is the underside of its body near the tail that is luminous. It is the female that makes this beautiful display, and her purpose is to attract the male, which is a winged and fully developed beetle, and so may reach her quickly even if he sees her light from afar.

An unpleasant feature of the roadside herbage in summer is the very remarkable cuckoo spit. Our ancestors were puzzled by the sudden appearance of this phenomenon, and without taking the trouble to examine it to find out the cause, they blamed it on the cuckoo because it first appears about the time that bird is most insistently announcing to the world at large that he is here. The cuckoo certainly has crimes to answer for, but this is not one of them.

The froth is caused by the larva of a plant insect belonging to the bug family. The full-grown insect is known as the frog-hopper, because when it is at rest its attitude is suggestive of that of a small frog, and because, though it has wings, it is much given to hopping and is capable of covering two or three feet at a single spring.

So far no one has been able to discover where this insect lays its eggs. They must be laid in summer or autumn, but the grubs do not hatch till next spring. As soon as one does, it takes up a position head downwards on the stalk of some

plant and feeds by sucking the sap. Presently it exudes a
clear syrupy liquid from its tail, and by beating this constantly with the hind part of its body, soon churns it into
froth. This lather increases so rapidly that in about an hour
it covers the whole insect, and so forms a most effective
protection against enemies.

The caterpillars of butterflies and moths also feed on
plants. They do not, however, suck the sap, but eat the
leaves or the wood. This accounts for the very ragged
appearance which so many leaves present as the summer
advances.

Some of our most beautiful butterflies feed as grubs on
the common stinging nettle, namely, the small tortoise-
shell, the peacock, the painted lady, the red admiral and the
Camberwell beauty. The commonest of them is the small
tortoiseshell. You may find its caterpillars on the under
sides of the nettle leaves in May and June, and again in July
and August, as there are two broods in the year. They are
black, speckled with yellow, and with a yellow line and a
row of yellow rings along each side, and are covered with
short yellowish hairs which have black tips.

When this caterpillar is full fed and so is ready to change
into a chrysalis, it spins a pad of silk on the under side of a
leaf stalk and hangs itself up to this by the tail. There it
remains quite still for several hours. Then its skin splits
and the head of the chrysalis begins to appear, and in three
or four minutes it is completely transformed into a helpless,
legless, mouthless and eyeless something which might pass
at a casual glance for a withered leaf, and is still hanging
by the tail. If you can watch it during those few minutes
you may see for yourself the solution of a problem which
puzzled naturalists for many years.

Before the creature can rid itself entirely of its cater-

The small tortoiseshell feeds as a grub on the common stinging nettle.

pillar skin, it has to withdraw its tail, and having done so it has to reach up and hook itself again to the pad of silk. At first this sounds like an impossible feat, because as the skin is stripped off from the head backwards, you would naturally think that when the tail was withdrawn the chrysalis would drop to the ground. What actually happens is that a small portion of the old skin still clings to the under side of the body while the tail is withdrawn, and thus provides support and leverage to enable the animal to raise itself and hook its new tail to the silk. As soon as that is accomplished, the chrysalis completes its sloughing by vigorous wriggling, and then hangs free till the time comes for the full-grown butterfly to emerge.

On the leaves of the ragwort, that very common yellow flower of the daisy family, you will find in July and August the caterpillar of the cinnabar moth. It is brilliantly marked with alternate bands of orange and black, and any-where else it would be very conspicuous. But in association with the yellow flowers and dark green ragged leaves of the ragwort it is almost invisible. So it has no need to hide behind the leaves as do the caterpillars of the small tortoise-shell butterfly. When it is full fed it drops to the ground, burrows just under the surface, and there changes into a chrysalis in which state it hibernates. The moth appears in the following June. It has vermilion hind wings and its forewings are greyish black, with a vermilion bar and two spots on each.

There is a host of wonders also among the plants of the wayside and wastes. For example, every one knows the common nettle and has been stung by it. Like the spines of thistle, gorse and holly, the sting is the plant's protection against browsing animals. Unfortunately the marvellous mechanism by which it is caused is too small to be seen by the naked eye. You cannot help noticing, however, that the surface of the leaves is covered with short, very fine hairs. If you examine these through a strong lens, you will see that each begins in a bulb on the skin of the leaf and ends in a tiny crooked knob. The upper part of the hair is brittle, and at the neck of the knob it is so weak that the lightest touch will break it. When that happens, a sharp ragged edge is left which will pierce the tender skin of a human being or the lips or tongue of a quadruped. The same touch presses the bulb, which is elastic and filled with poison, and so instantaneously squeezes its contents into the wound. So, except for the knob, the sting of a nettle is similar to the poison fang of a snake. It is strange that the same apparatus should have been evolved by two such widely diverse creatures, the one for defence and the other for attack, and that it should also long afterwards have been invented by man as the hypodermic syringe for surgical purposes.

Very often you will notice a plant with conspicuous white flowers growing in the middle of a patch of nettles. Its leaves are similar in form to those of the nettle, but they are not provided with stings. This is the white deadnettle. It belongs to an entirely different family, as you will readily understand if you compare its blossoms with the minute yellowish green flowers of the common nettle. Its resemblance to the nettle is its only defence. So long as it grows in company with that plant it is perfectly safe, because it will escape notice except when its flowers are in bloom, but when it springs up separately its likeness to the nettle must deceive browsing animals and so often save its life.

The blossom of this plant is remarkable for its form, and the reason for that form is very wonderful. You will notice that the petals are united to form a tube as in the

case of the primrose. Unlike the primrose, however, th
mouth of this tube is not open to the skies. Its rim i
peculiarly cut into two prominent lips, one of which i
arched above the mouth like a hood and the other thrus
out below like a protruding tongue. Underneath the hoo
you will find the two true flowers, which are thus effectivel
protected from rain and hidden from insects. Insects, how
ever, do visit the blossom, and the under lip is invitingl
offered to them as a convenient landing place. But withi
the throat there is a ring of hairs which prevents smal
insects from crawling down into the tube and stealing th
honey. Such visitors are of no value to the plant, and it
honey is intended for those that will render it a service i
return for the delicious gift. Bumble bees have long tongue
which they can thrust through the hairy palisade and s
reach the sweet store, and as they sip it their furry back
brush the flowers hidden under the hood. Thus they carr
the fertilising pollen from blossom to blossom and plant t
plant, and so pay in transport for the food they have taken

The remarkable two-lipped blossom of the dead nettl
family is specially designed to suit the bumble bee. Th
common nettle grows its two flowers on separate plants
and they are fertilised by the wind. The red campion an
the ragged robin, which are so common on waysides every
where, have deep tubes which are rifled by long-tongue
butterflies, and the white campion of the fields and th
honeysuckle of the hedges, which open their blossoms firs
in the evening, appeal specially to night-flying moths
Many plants, however, are content with the services of flie
and beetles, and among them are the umbrella flowers o
the hemlock family and the shallow open flowers of th
rose family.

The hemlock family is a large one and many of its

members are difficult to identify. The hemlock itself is a tall plant with a smooth stem which is spotted with purple. Other members of the family are similarly spotted, but it is easy to distinguish the hemlock from them by the fact that it is the only one with short fruits. One of the commonest species is the cow parsnip or hogweed. Its coarse, hairy, hollow stems are often used by boys for making peashooters. Another very plentiful species is the wild carrot, and the family also includes species with such names as hedge parsley, sweet cicely, angelica, etc. They all produce bunches of very small flowers which separately would hardly attract attention, but bear them on stalks of equal length and display them in such a manner that they form an almost continuous flat surface like the top of a Japanese umbrella. Flies and beetles alight on these and run here and there on them sipping the honey, and as they do so they carry pollen from one blossom to another on their legs and bodies. On the hogweed you will notice that the blossoms on the outermost ring of each bunch are larger than the rest, and that their outer petals are the largest. Like the white rays of the daisy, this helps to make the bunch as a whole more conspicuous. The wild carrot is easily recognised by the fact that in the centre of each of its white umbrellas there is a single red blossom. In spite of its colour this one tinted flower cannot increase the attractiveness of the bunch to passing insects, but once they have alighted it may arouse their curiosity and so induce them to cross the umbrella.

The cuckoo-pint, or lords and ladies or wild arum as it is variously called, makes use of small flies in a much more ingenious way. Its flowers are hidden by its large yellowish-green leaf called a "spathe" which is wrapped round them like a shawl upside down, but it attracts visitors by means

of the long red club-like end of its stalk. The insects make
their way down into the interior of the tube formed by the
spathe, through a palisade of hairs which allows them to
enter but not to return. Inside this trap there are two sets
of flowers growing one above the other round the stalk
The lower group are the seed makers. They are ripe first
and they provide a supply of honey for the prisoners which
if they have previously visited another arum, bring with
them the magic pollen which will enable the plant to produce fertile seed. When these flowers have withered, the
upper bunch comes to maturity and sheds a shower of
pollen, some of which falls on and clings to the imprisoned
flies. Then the palisade of hairs withers and sets the prisoners
free to carry the precious dust to another plant.

This is one of the plants that produce berries. The red
club and the spathe wither away, and nothing is left but a
stump of the stalk surmounted by a closely packed bunch of
green berries which later become red. These fruits, however, are poisonous to man.

It is the rose family that supplies most of our edible
fruits, and many and varied they are. From the strawberry
to the apple, they are so strikingly varied that it is difficult
at first to believe that they are so closely related. But if
you examine the plants themselves from the lowliest to the
highest, you will notice how constant the flowers are in
form and how, in spite of considerable modifications, the
family likeness is retained in the leaves.

The strawberry and the barren strawberry are common
on waysides and wastes. Their leaves are very much alike,
but when they are in flower or fruit they are easily identified.
The petals of the strawberry are rounded at the tip whereas
those of the barren strawberry are notched, and instead of
bearing juicy domes speckled with seeds, the latter plant

produces only a bunch of dry seeds. Other common wayside roses are the cinquefoil, silverweed, wood avens and agrimony, all of which have yellow blossoms. The cinquefoil you may know by its five-fingered leaves, the silverweed by its long prostrate leaves with their many silvery leaflets. The wood avens and the agrimony show that the genius of the family was not limited to the invention of berries. Both provide their seeds with little hooks by which they cling to passing animals, and so are carried about till they drop. Each seed of the avens has a long hook to itself, but the agrimony, which can be recognised by the fact that it consists of a single tall stem spangled along the greater part of its length with little yellow, five-rayed stars, encloses its seeds in a small oblong nut which has a ring of hooks round one end.

The second set of violet flowers, which never open and are never visited by insects, nevertheless develop a plentiful supply of seeds. When these are ripe, the case containing them breaks into three sections which spread out horizontally, and then by pinching the pellets, shoot them to a distance of many feet.

The method of distributing seeds employed in the large daisy family, which includes daisies, dandelions and thistles, is by means of downy parachutes which are blown away by the wind and carry their precious burdens with them. Every one knows the wonderful dandelion clocks, but very few, not even the writers of books on wild flowers, seem to have noticed a still more remarkable characteristic of this common plant. Each dandelion head contains between two and three hundred separate florets, each with a yellow ribbon, honey, and seed-making organs of its own. They are not all, however, in bloom at the same time. They come to maturity in rings beginning at the circumference and ending at the centre. This process occupies three or four days during which the head is visited by many insects. Each day the head opens early in the morning and closes in the evening but after the fourth evening it does not expand again till the seeds are ready to fly.

Then begins a series of movements which are among the great miracles of the countryside but which, because they are slow and are performed by a withered and apparently dead flower, are passed by unobserved. The tall, hollow stem of the dandelion first bends about an inch below the neck so that the head is tilted slightly inwards. Then it bends in the opposite direction about an inch above the root and gradually lowers itself till its curved neck is resting on the ground. There it remains for about ten days, during which period the seeds are ripened and their delicate parachutes are developed. Then it begins to unbend and slowly rises till, when it finally straightens its neck, it is as upright as it was when it was in bloom, and is ready to expand its beautiful ball of down.

I have noticed that when a dandelion plant grows on open ground its various flower stalks, when lowered for seed-making, form a rosette. When, however, it grows at the foot of a wall or a steep bank, those stalks on the inner side do not rest against the perpendicular obstruction as you would expect them to do, plants being in our conception purely mechanical organisms, but instead, reverse their curves and lie across the plant. This suggests that they are sensitive. Without touching the wall they seem to be aware of its undesirable presence, and not only that, but by adopting revolutionary measures they are able to avoid it and so accomplish their end.

Similar movements are practised by the common wayside geranium called herb Robert, but as the flowers and their stalks are so much smaller than those of the dandelion, the changes are not so noticeable. If you examine the plant, however, you will see that the buds hang down till the time for blossoming arrives, and then they become erect. When the flower withers, the stalk droops until the seeds are ripe, and then it rises upright again. Meanwhile a long sharp spike, like the beak of a wading bird, has grown out from the middle of the flower cup. From this curious growth the geranium family gets its popular name of cranesbill. It is not simply curious or ornamental, however, but is a very ingenious and practical contrivance. Around its base you will find five little lumps. Each of these contains a seed, and the only opening by which it can escape is pressed tight against the bill. Presently the outer skin of the bill splits from top to bottom into five strips, each of which is attached to one of the seed cases and so forms with it a tiny ladle. As it dries the ladle contracts and the handle becomes taut, till at last the strain is so great that it springs out from below and, using the top of the bill as a fulcrum, throws itself away from the plant, turning a somersault as it does so. At the same moment the seed escapes and is sent flying to a distance of several feet, where it rests till next spring.

CHAPTER EIGHT

MARSHES AND MOORS

ON open marshy land almost anywhere you will find the snipe in spring and summer. You may be attracted first by his peculiar mating call, which is known as "drumming," but is remarkably like the bleating of a goat. When you do hear that note, look up in the air and watch the movements of a bird you will see circling there with very rapid wing beats. You will notice that now and then he dives, then rises again and circles on now this way now that. Every time he plunges he bleats, and he never makes this call at any other part of his manœuvres. For long it was believed that he uttered this note with his voice, but the fact that it was heard only when he was engaged in his aerial dance suggested that the sound was caused by his rapidly moving wings. It has now been proved, however, that the bleating is due to the vibrations of the two outermost feathers of his tail during his swift dive. While this is in progress the tail is full spread, and the outermost feather on each side is held quite apart from the rest. These two feathers are more rigid and more closely knit than the others and it is they that cause the sound. If the snipe rises at your feet when you are crossing marsh or moor, you will recognise him by the curious note he utters which sounds like *snape*, and by his erratic zigzag flight.

The snipe belongs to the wader family which, as their name implies, are specially adapted for living on marshy or boggy land or on the seashore. They have long legs which enable them to wade easily in more or less shallow water or to move about freely on soft mud, and this is so much their habit that their feet have become unsuited for perching, the hind toe being either very small or altogether missing. Their food consists of worms, slugs, grubs, snails, sand-hoppers and so on and in order that they may capture such prey, many of the species are provided with long bills by means of which they may reach the bottom of pools, or snap at creatures swimming below the surface, or probe deep in the mud.

The snipe is specially fond of worms. He has a very long straight bill, and his head is so poised that he is able to drive this weapon perpendicularly into the ground. I have watched him at work and have never seen him miss his prey, and at the same time I have been astonished at the large number of worms he is able to dispose of in a short time.

The woodcock is similar in form to the snipe, but is much larger. He also makes his living by probing in marshy land, but he works only by night and spends his days resting in some wood which may be a considerable distance from his feeding place. There he sits on the ground, and his plumage so closely resembles his surroundings that you may pass within a yard of him and never see him. At dusk, however, he rouses himself and silently makes for the open, flitting cautiously low down along some ride till he reaches the edge of the wood, and then, abruptly mounting high in the air, he flies swiftly and straight to the marsh. He returns at dawn, employing the same tactics in the reverse order. He is so regular in his habits that, if you once see a woodcock leave a wood in the twilight you may be sure of seeing him doing the same thing at the same spot and about the same time on every subsequent evening. Moreover, if several woodcock inhabit the same wood, they will all probably leave by the same route at short intervals.

Woodcock also nest in woods, so when the young are hatched the necessity of feeding them presents a serious problem to the parents, but they solve it in an original way. Instead of fetching food every few minutes to the waiting family as other birds do, they carry the helpless chicks to the marsh and feed them there. Thus they save themselves much time and many journeys.

It has now been established that the woodcock carries its young in various ways, sometimes in its bill, sometimes on its back, but most commonly between the legs—which in flight are pressed against the body—with support occasionally from the long bill or from the tail feathers which can be depressed and held partly under the burden. Few have witnessed these interesting operations, however, so every new record of them would be a valuable contribution towards our knowledge of the bird.

On upland marshes and moors in spring and summer you are sure to see the curlew, another wader. He is a large bird with a bill six or more inches long which curves downward towards the tip. Unsuitable as this instrument may seem for the purpose, it is, none the less, used for extracting worms from the depths of their burrows. The best place, however, to watch the feeding of the curlew is a sandy or muddy seashore where he spends the autumn and winter months. The bill of the young curlew for the first few weeks of its life is short and straight.

The curlew is remarkable also for his beautiful spring song and for the manner in which he delivers it. He mounts thirty or forty feet in the air and then, while planing gently down to the ground on steady wings, he sings a long, plaintive trill which is wonderfully characteristic of the wild and desolate country in which he lives. His usual call consists of two notes, *wha-up*, the second being considerably higher than the first.

On the moors also, but still more on lowland marshes, you will find another very common wader, the redshank. He is one of the commonest, wildest and most attractive of all the marsh birds. You will recognise him by his red legs and red bill if you can get close enough to see them, but he is so wary that at first you are more likely to see him in flight and to hear his beautiful call, *tyu-hu, tyu-hu-hu*, which is touched with a haunting melancholy, as if the performer were deeply affected by the intense loneliness of his native solitudes. As he flies away from you, you will notice his white rump and a broad white bar across his wings.

He is always a very excitable bird, and when he is alarmed his call often develops into a long series of notes which is almost hysterical. In spring, he becomes quite frenzied, and often gives expression to his feelings by hovering about thirty feet from the ground on outstretched wings which are held almost stiff except at the tips, and repeating rapidly a single note. Then as he planes to the ground he sings his joyful love song, *te-leera, te-leera, te-leera*.

He is very frequently to be seen on the muddy shores of ditch or stream, either standing still, probably asleep, or stepping about quietly and picking up tit-bits. But he is at his very best when he is wading more than knee deep in the water in active pursuit of his favourite prey, small shrimp-like creatures which he snaps up briskly as they dart near him.

The golden plover is a bird of the moorlands in spring and summer and of the lowland marshes in autumn and winter, and if you know him in the one you will hardly recognise him if you meet him unexpectedly in the other. His summer dress is black and gold speckle above and solid black on neck, breast and under parts, the two colourings being separated by a broad white band that begins on the forehead, and passes over the eye, down the sides of the neck and under the wings. In winter these white and black zones disappear and are replaced by speckling on the breast and white underneath. At this season he lives in flocks which often feed in company with lapwings. If they are disturbed at such times the two species at once separate, and then the golden plover are easily distinguished, apart from their colour, by their sharp curved wings and rapid flight. Their common call in summer consists of two long-drawn, melancholy notes, *too—tee*, with a distinct interval between them, and in winter a beautiful liquid single note which can only be suggested by the syllable *tlee*. The cock also has a spring song which may be described as *taludl-taludl-taludl*.

Another wader of the moorlands is the common sand-piper. You will see him there on the shores of streams and lochs. He is a small bird, about an inch shorter than the starling, but with longer legs than that species. You will know him by the fact that when he is disturbed he flies out over the water, skimming close to the surface and piping

repeatedly his thin, high-pitched call which sounds like
tee-tee-tee. His colouring is brown above and white underneath, with a bold white band across his outstretched wings
and a white feather on each side of his tail. When he is on
the shore he has a habit of bobbing like a robin.

He is only a summer visitor to this country, but from
mid-July to October you may see him on lowland marshes.
There you will usually come upon him unexpectedly in a
ditch, but even then he will not fly up and away as other
birds would do. True to his nature, he will skim along the
water or mud and flash round the next corner before you
have time to note his colouring. But he will settle not far
off, so by careful stalking you will usually find him again.

The heron is a wader and yet not a wader. He does not
belong to the wader family, but he is built on similar lines
to that group of birds, and he wades for his living. You will
see him on any lowland marsh usually in the ditches, and
also on the margins of streams and ponds and on the seashore. Where the bed shelves quickly, he wades in up to the
knees and stands waiting for fish or other suitable morsels
to swim within his reach. Then he lowers his head and,
plunging it suddenly into the water, makes his capture.
But where the pond or stream is shallow he wades about
in search of prey, and then his character, which in other
circumstances seems to be slow and sluggish, changes and
he shows himself to be an active and enterprising bird.

You will recognise him on the ground by his long grey
neck and crested head ; when in flight he tucks them well
back between his shoulders, but then you will know him
at a glance by his great slowly flapping wings and his long
legs which are held straight out behind him.

There is one species of bird which is to be found in the
British Isles and nowhere else in the world, namely, the red

grouse. It inhabits the moors, and is hardy enough to live there all the year round. In form it is like the partridge but it is larger than that species and is reddish brown in colour. Like the partridge also, it lives in pairs in summer and in coveys during the winter. It is very plentiful, and as you cross the moors you will probably put up many individuals. Even when you do not see it you will hear the peculiar crowing of the cocks, which always ends with *go-back, go-back, go-back, back, back*.

Where woods adjoin the moors you may have the good luck to see the blackcock, a very handsome bird belonging to the same family. The cock is glossy blue-black and has a beautiful lyre-shaped tail. He roosts in trees like the pheasant but feeds on the moors, and like the pheasant he goes in parties, one cock mating with several hens.

One of the very first of our summer visitors is the ring ouzel, a cousin of our common blackbird. When he arrives about the middle of March, he makes at once for the moors where he spends the spring and summer. He is all black like his cousin except for a broad white crescent on his breast, so the name ring ouzel does not describe him accurately. He differs from the blackbird also in having a dark, instead of an orange, bill.

About the middle of March also the little wheatear, another member of the thrush family, arrives, and takes possession of his territory on marshes, moors and other waste ground. His plumage is blue-grey above with black wings and tail, white rump and chestnut breast, and he has a black stripe above his eye. It is important to remember about the white rump, because as he flits along before you, this is very conspicuous and enables you to identify him. He is not at all shy, however, but rather curious like the robin, and though he will keep out of reach, he will sit on

Where woods adjoin the moors you may have the good luck to see the blackcock.

a stone or clod of earth and watch you as you advance towards him, bobbing and flicking his tail the while.

Where marshy ground is covered with scrub, you will hear in May and June the very remarkable song of the grasshopper warbler. This name describes the note very well, but it will help you to identify it if you think of the sound made by a fishing reel being wound quickly, or of a lawn mower being worked two or three gardens away. There is just a suggestion of a whistle in the sound which softens it and makes it pleasing to the ear. You may hear this little songster best in the evening about dusk when he reels incessantly, often sustaining the note for more than two minutes. He is difficult to see, because it is his habit to skulk among bushes and undergrowth, but if you do see him when he is not singing, you will be able to distinguish him from other warblers by the fact that his tail has a rounded tip.

Where there is such a large bird population there must be many deaths, but it is remarkable how seldom you will meet with evidence of them. Nature provides scavengers here as elsewhere, and one of the commonest of them is the carrion crow. Of course you will find him in other parts as well, even in London, but he is so much a feature of the marshlands that it is best to deal with him here. It is easy to distinguish a crow from a rook in pictures, because the rook has a conspicuous patch of white skin at the base of his beak and the crow hasn't. But it is not so simple in real life, for young rooks and newly moulted adults do not have the white patch, and besides sunlight striking on a crow's beak often gives the semblance of a white patch where there is none. When you see the birds singly or in pairs they are more likely to be crows than rooks, but rooks often fly singly and crows sometimes go in flocks. So frequently the

only sure sign by which to distinguish the two is the call.
The rook utters a deep caw, which is usually single. The
crow as a rule repeats his note three times. It is harsh, and
sounds like *carr-carr-carr.*

The conditions of life on the marshes have affected
plants as well as birds. A large number of plants are to be
found only on marshy ground, and this fact is often indicated in their names. Thus we have marsh marigold, marsh
violet, marsh cinquefoil, marsh thistle, marsh speedwell,
bog asphodel, bog myrtle and so on.

One of the most interesting of all the marsh plants, and
one of the most wonderful plants in this country, is the
purple loosestrife. It is quite common and is very conspicuous, for it is tall, often as much as five feet in height,
grows in thick clumps and bears many large purple star-like
blossoms, which are arranged in closely packed circles on
the upper part of the stem. It is because of these blossoms
that the species is so wonderful. If you examine a number
of the plants you will find that they differ. The blossoms
may have four, five or six petals, but that is not important.
It is the true flowers within them that matter, and they are
grown in three different combinations. The seed-forming
flower, or style as it is called, is single, but it may be short,
or long or of medium length. The pollen-making flowers,
or stamens, are many and are also produced in three sizes,
two of which are in each blossom in separate groups.
Where the style is (*a*) short, the two clusters of stamens are
medium and long; where it is (*b*) medium, they are short
and long; and where it is (*c*) long, they are short and
medium. So a blossom can be fertilised only by an insect
that brings pollen from another on that part of its body
which will come in contact with the style. Thus one of the
first group, *a*, can be fertilised by pollen from the other

two, *b* and *c*, one of the *b* group by pollen from *a* and *c*, and one of the *c* group by pollen from *a* and *b*. The short style and stamens would brush against the head of a bee, the medium against her thorax and the long against her abdomen.

There is another marsh plant called the yellow loose-strife. This species, however, is not in any way related to the purple loosestrife. It belongs to the same family as the primrose. Like that plant, it has two forms of flower which are fertilised only by a particular species of bee. This bee is uncommon, and curiously enough, it is to be found only in neighbourhoods where the yellow loosestrife grows. It is a black insect with its thorax clothed with short brownish hairs.

Very few flowers in this country are visited by wasps. Figwort, a plant of marshy ground, is one of them. Now when a bee visits a plant she begins, like the tree creeper on the trunk of a tree, at the bottom and works upwards. Whether this is her original method or is a habit induced by the fact that most plants open their lowest blossoms first and their uppermost ones last, it is impossible to say now, but it is curious that when a wasp does seek honey from a plant, it starts at the top and works downwards. So a plant that opened its higher blossoms first would benefit by the attentions of a wasp provided its style were ripe before its pollen, for then the pollen of the upper flowers would be carried to the styles of the lower ones or to those of another plant which had come into bloom later. The figwort does this partly. Its style ripens before its pollen, and its blossoms open in no regular order, so they are better suited to the erratic visits of the wasp than to the methodical progression of the bee. Its petals are joined to form a little globe of a pale greenish-purple tint, but the upper part of the rim is extended into a long protruding up-curving lip which is coloured reddish-brown.

Among the heather and cottongrass of the moors you will find two very remarkable plants, the sundew and the butterwort. The sundew is a curious little plant with round leaves on long stalks about the size and shape of salt spoons. The leaves are green, but they are covered with hundreds of red hairs. On sunny days the tip of each hair glistens as if it carried a tiny drop of dew. But no matter how hot the day may be, this dew does not dry up. If you touch it lightly with your finger you will find that it is really a sticky fluid like gum. Any small insect that alights on the leaves is caught and held tight by this adhesive dew, and the more it struggles the more the fluid is poured out until it is drowned. Then its body is digested by the juice as it would be in the stomach of an animal, and absorbed by the leaf.

The butterwort, which lives in boggy ground on upland moors, is also an insect eater. It is sometimes called the bog violet because its flowers, which are hung up each on a tall stalk, are similar in colour and also to some extent in form to those of the violet, though this species belongs to another family. But the leaves are the most interesting part of the plant. They are thick, green, oval and stalkless, and they are spread out on the ground in the form of a rosette. Their edges are turned up and their surface glistens with a film of gum, which is poured out by a large number of tiny hairs. Insects are attracted to them either by their glitter or by their musty odour, and alight on them to sip the honey-like juice; but the viscid surface grips their feet and, try how they may, they cannot escape. Then the edges of the leaf turn inwards and close over the victim like the skin of a sea anemone. Thereupon other hairs pour out a digestive

liquid which dissolves all but the hardest parts of the body,
and the juice thus obtained is absorbed into the leaf. Seeds,
pollen and other kinds of food are dealt with in the same
way, but, strange to tell, though the leaf is stirred into
activity by the tiniest midge or plant cell, it takes no notice
of a grain of sand. It is able to distinguish between what is
food and what is not.

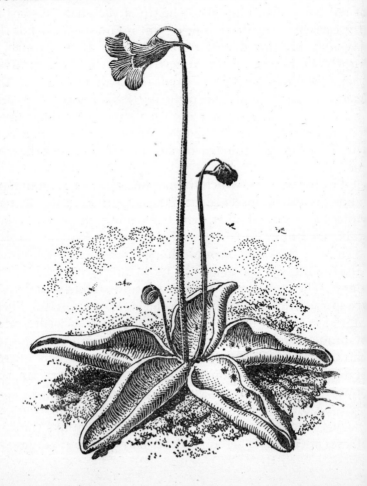

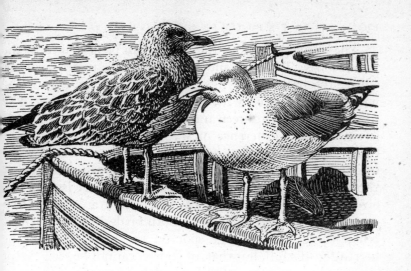

CHAPTER NINE

THE COAST

ONE of the best places in which to observe the gulls is a harbour, for there you often get quite close views of them. There they may alight on a buoy or a post or swim close to the quay; or they may fly round some boat, waiting for scraps to be thrown into the water, and when that happens will all make a dash for the spot and scramble for the tit-bits.

Now, whenever you see a gull standing anywhere you should always look first at its legs and make a note of their colour. For if you don't do this at once, the bird may fly away while you are examining its head and body, and then you will not be able to see its legs at all, though you may study its plumage so long as it is within sight. You will understand the importance of this hint when you are trying to decide whether a bird is a common gull or a herring-gull.

The plumage of both these birds can be described in the same words. The head and neck and all the under parts are white, the back and wings are light grey, the tips of the wings black spotted with white, and the tail white. The common gull is eighteen inches long and the herring-gull twenty-four, a difference of six inches, which you might think was quite enough to make identification easy. And so it would be if the two birds were close together so that you could compare their sizes. But when there is only one bird, or when two or more are widely separated, it is often impossible to judge by inches. Both birds also have yellow bills; there is an orange spot on the lower half of the herring-gull's bill, but that, of course, cannot be seen except at very close quarters. The legs of the common gull, how-ever, are greenish-yellow, while those of the herring-gull are flesh-coloured.

The lesser black-backed gull is just about the same size as the herring-gull, but can never be mistaken for it because its back and wings are black, and its legs are yellow. The greater black-backed gull, however, is very similar to the lesser and, though it is seven inches longer, its size is only a trustworthy guide when the two birds are close enough to be compared. But again the colour of the legs is distinctive. The greater black-backed gull has flesh-coloured legs, and the lesser, as I have already said, has yellow legs.

The black-headed gull and the kittiwake are just about the same size as the common gull, but the former has red and the latter blackish, legs. The kittiwake also has no white spots on the black tips of its wings.

At all times it is easy to identify the black-headed gull if you can see its head clearly, though this is not always black. Indeed, it is never black, but in spring and summer it is chocolate, and thus at a distance looks black. It is important to note that this colouring forms a kind of hood covering the chin and throat as well as the head.

In August this hood begins to disappear, so then you may see some black-headed gulls with chocolate heads, some with heads spotted brown and white, and some with heads that are all white but for two small brown spots on each side, one before and the other behind the eye. This last is the marking by which you will recognise the species throughout the winter.

But there are other grey and white sea birds with black heads and red legs which on that account may be confused with the black-headed gull. This time, however, the heads are really black, and the colour is only on the top and back and not on the cheeks or neck. These birds are the terns or sea swallows. They are not true swallows, but are so called because their long pointed wings and forked tails give them a swallow-like form. It is by this form that you may know them most readily.

There are several species of tern and four of them are so very much alike that it is almost impossible to distinguish them apart except by the colour of the bill. The common tern has a red bill with a black tip. The bill of the Arctic tern is blood red all over. These two resemble each other most closely, and it is often impossible to see the colour of the bill, so when you do identify one of them you should make a careful study of its calls and memorise them, for by them you will most readily recognise the species at all times. The Arctic tern, as its name shows, is a more northern species than the common, but it nests in the Scilly Isles, the Isle of Man, Lancashire, Anglesey, and the Farne Isles. It is much the more abundant in Scotland, especially on the north-west coast.

The roseate tern gets its name from the fact that its

breast is tinted with rose pink. This, however, is not a reliable feature by which to identify it, because the Sandwich tern has a flush of salmon pink on its breast, and even the common tern sometimes shows a slight tinge of pink on this part of its plumage. So again you must make sure of the colouring of the bill to be quite certain of the species. In this instance it is black. There is some red at the base but this is hardly noticeable except at very close quarters.

The Sandwich tern is a larger bird than these three, and its tail is shorter than theirs and not so deeply forked. Its bill is black with a yellow tip, and its feet are black, whereas theirs are red.

The little tern is smaller than the others and has orange bill and legs, but its most distinctive feature is a conspicuous white spot on its forehead.

In spring and autumn you may also see black terns. You will recognise them by the darker grey of their upper parts.

But there are still other birds that will add to your difficulties. These are not separate species but young of those species already mentioned, and each kind has a special juvenile plumage of its own. For example, the young black headed gull is like its parents in their winter dress, except that it has brown on its wings, a black bar across the tip of its tail, and yellowish-red legs, and its bill is dusky instead of red. The young herring-gull and lesser black backed gull are mottled brown and white, and are so much alike that it is impossible to say to which species they belong.

Another way by which you may know the terns is their method of feeding. They fly along about fifteen or twenty feet above the water, hover for a little, then plunge right into the sea, capture a small fish and fly up again. The gulls, on the other hand, drop to the surface and pick up tit-bits that may be floating there, but do not dive.

A far more wonderful diver than the terns is the gannet or solan goose. This is a large white bird with conspicuous black tips to its wings. It floats along at a great height, then suddenly closes its wings and falls like a bolt into the sea with a great splash, captures and swallows a herring or a mackerel and then flies up to resume its watch.

The gannet is neither a gull nor a tern, and it is not even a goose though it is called solan goose, and goose is what gannet means. Its nearest relatives are the cormorant and the shag, which are as different as possible from it in appearance. They are large black birds with long thin necks and hooked beaks. The cormorant is the larger of the two and has a white patch on its throat and on each side in spring. They dive, but from the surface instead of from the air. They swim so low in the water that it is often difficult to see them because only the neck and head are visible. As they pursue their prey under water they do not come up where they dive, but often at a considerable distance from that spot. When they capture a fish they bring it to the surface and swallow it there, and sometimes the victim is so large that they are able to gulp it down only with the greatest difficulty.

When they are satisfied, they fly to some rock to rest, and there they hang themselves out to dry, with their wings outstretched like clothes on a line and their mouths wide open as if they had eaten far too much.

Two other birds belonging to quite a different family may easily be mistaken for the cormorant by beginners, namely the guillemot and the razorbill which are also chiefly swimmers and divers. They are only about half the size of the cormorant, however, and though they are dark above (the razorbill is black and the guillemot dark brown,

which looks black at a distance) they are both white under
neath. Besides, the cormorant will come right into
harbour to feed and will fish in quite shallow water, bu
you will see the other two only in deep water, except in th
nesting season when they sit up on rocks like little penguins
They make no nest, but each hen lays one large egg on
bare ledge of rock. So close together are these eggs place
that you cannot help wondering how each mother recognise
her own. The razorbill, however, is the more carefu
mother of the two, for she lays her egg as a rule in hole
or crevices of the cliff or on ledges sheltered by overhangin
rock. The guillemot, on the other hand, takes no troubl
to protect hers from the weather, but lays it on an expose
ledge, or on the flat top of a tall sea stack.

Another difference between the two birds is the manne
in which they brood the egg. The guillemot sits uprigh
on hers, holding it on the top of her webbed feet, wherea
the razorbill snuggles down like the majority of birds.

One of the marvels of nature is how the young razorbill
and guillemots reach the sea. They are hatched on precipice
hundreds of feet above it, and yet they are seen swimmin
with their mothers long before they can fly. Fishermen sa
that they are carried down on the backs or in the mouths o
their parents, but this has not been proved, and som
observers have seen them flying without aid. The chic
plunges from the ledge and though his wings are not stron
enough to support him, spreads and flaps them, and thu
steadies himself in his descent. They even help him t
guide himself to some extent and they break the shock o
his arrival. And when he reaches the water, he is able t
dive and swim with ease in the heavy breakers which ar
dashing against the cliff. He is immediately joined by hi
parents who lead him out to sea, and he and they spend th

winter, the season of storms and bitter cold, somewhere on the Atlantic.

The guillemot has a long, sharply-pointed bill. The razorbill, as its name implies, has a beak so narrow that it looks as if its edge might be used for cutting. This beak is also short and deep and rounded at the tip. It has one or more white lines running across it from top to bottom, and there is another straight white line which passes back from its top to the eye. The razorbill also has a distinct white bar on each wing. A peculiarity of these birds is that they paddle with their webbed feet when they are on the surface but when they are under water they swim with their wings and use their legs as rudders.

The puffin is a smaller member of this family, but is easily recognised by his large, narrow beak, which resembles a pair of short shears, but is brilliantly coloured with alternate bands of bright red and orange. The puffin breeds in large colonies like its cousins, and the hen is an even more prudent mother than the razorbill. She invariably lays her egg in a hole, and usually in a burrow under turf. Frequently she commandeers a rabbit burrow, attacking the owner and driving it out if it dares to object, but failing this, she digs a tunnel for herself.

When you visit an island where puffins, guillemots and razorbills nest, you will notice another remarkable difference between the three species. The puffin stands up on its toes like most other birds. The guillemot and the razorbill, however, are unable to do this, but sit upright with the whole foot (that is, the leg to the first joint which is really the heel) resting on the rock.

All three species feed their young on fish. The guillemot swallows his prey and disgorges it when he reaches the home ledge, but the razorbill and the puffin carry theirs to the nest in their bills, about half a dozen at a time, arranged in a neat row with the heads and tails pointing alternately right and left.

The black guillemot which nests on the west coast from the Isle of Man northwards, on the north coast of Scotland, and in Orkney and Shetland, is easily distinguished from the common guillemot by the fact that its plumage is all black with the exception of a large white patch on each wing. This species does not nest in such vast colonies as the other. A few pairs may breed, more or less, in company, and the hen, like the cautious razorbill, usually lays her egg in a cranny of a cliff or under a boulder.

Where there are caves in the rocky cliffs you may see the rock dove or blue rock. This is the species from which all our fancy pigeons have been bred. It nests and roosts in these caves, and when it leaves their shelter, it dashes out swiftly as if it fears that some enemy is waiting to pounce when it appears at the entrance. The rock dove is smaller than the wood pigeon, and does not have white on the upper side of the wings or on the neck.

The stock dove is also common where it can find nesting holes in the rocky cliffs. It is similar in size and plumage to the rock dove, but you may recognise them apart by the fact that the rock is white on the rump and under the wings, and the stock dove grey.

The hereditary enemy of these birds is the peregrine falcon which also nests on rocky cliffs. This large, handsome bird, when he is not hunting, will sit for hours on some favourite crag which he uses as a look-out post, and his breast, which is white, barred with black, is then often very conspicuous against the dark background.

But you may often see him at play either alone or with his mate. The game consists in mounting high in the air over the sea and then suddenly "stooping," that is, half-closing the wings and shooting down like a bolt, but, just when you are expecting him to plunge into the water, turning sharply, skimming the surface for a short distance, then rising again in preparation for another dive. He is at his very best, however, when he is actually in pursuit of prey. Then there is magnificent dash in his swift, purposeful flight. He quickly overtakes his intended victim, rising high above it so as to gain impetus for his blow, and when he reaches the proper strategic position he stoops. Down he goes like a bomb, with incredible speed and a great hissing of air, and strikes his prey on the back with his spurs, then rises suddenly, checks his speed and returns at leisure to enjoy his meal. The stricken bird is killed instantaneously and falls to the ground.

On sandy or muddy shores, and especially in estuaries where the receding tide leaves wide stretches of mudflats, you will find good hunting ground. Very few birds are there in summer, but in autumn and winter many species of waders come to feed there. These birds are related to the terns and seagulls, but do not have webbed feet, so, instead of swimming, content themselves with paddling about in the pools and at the edge of the sea, or with seeking food on mud or sand when the tide is out.

At all seasons you may see the ringed plover on sandy and shingly shores, for it nests there in summer. But the best time to study the waders is from August to March. Then curlew, redshank, and golden plover leave the moorlands and resort to the seaside where they feed at low tide on the mudflats, and other species come from the far north to winter on our coasts. At this season the dunlin gather in large flocks, and frequently you may see a number of ringed plover feeding and flying in company with them.

You may know the ringed plover by the fact that it has a broad white collar with a broad black collar under it, also a black bandeau across the head from eye to eye with a bold white patch right in the middle of the forehead. It has a short bill, whereas the dunlin has a long, straight black bill. In summer the dunlin has a large black patch on the lower part of the breast, and if you see a flock early in August you will probably notice that some of the birds are still wearing this decoration.

These birds are very restless, or rather impulsive. A flock alights on the mud and trots about seeking food. While so engaged the individuals gradually become scattered, but suddenly and apparently without reason, they rise simultaneously, close ranks quickly and are off in a compact flock. They fly hither and thither, wheeling and turning, their white under parts flashing beautifully as they do so, with wonderful skill and precision, and uttering their sweet, liquid, plaintive calls as they go. Then suddenly they alight again and proceed with their feeding, or rest for a while. I think these frequent flights must be an instinctive plan to keep the flock together, but whatever they may be, they are very beautiful and inspiring to the beholder.

Snipe come to the mudflats to feed in the late afternoon and evening and set to work the moment they alight. The purpose of their very long straight bills then becomes evident. They are as active as starlings in their search, stepping about smartly and turning their heads sharply from side to side. Then when one finds a burrow in which a worm is lurking, he stands over it, draws in his chin and drives his bill straight down into the mud to the very hilt. A moment later he drags forth a long, wriggling worm which he swallows immediately, and then he hurries off fussily to look for another.

*They fly hither and thither, wheeling and turning, their white
underparts flashing.*

The oyster-catcher, a much larger member of the family, which you will recognise by his handsome black and white plumage and his bright red bill and legs, frequently feeds in a similar way. But when he does so he is much more deliberate about it. He walks slowly about the beach inspecting anything and everything, and now and again probes in the mud. This he does quite casually, and when he captures a worm he shows no excitement about it, but calmly carries it a pace or two, lays it down, turns it over as if to examine it, and then picks it up and swallows it.

The favourite food of this bird, however, is shellfish. He is an expert at opening mussels and knocking limpets from their hold. If you take hold of a limpet and try to drag it from its rock you will not succeed, for the more you pull, the tighter he will grip. When the oyster-catcher fancies a limpet, however, he goes up to it calmly, strikes it a sudden sidelong blow with his strong beak, and over it rolls at his feet.

The long curved bill of the curlew seems a most unsuitable instrument for probing, but I have seen it so used repeatedly, and have been astonished at the rapidity with which the thick lug-worms vanish into it. Here is a mystery. It is easy to understand how the snipe and the oyster-catcher succeed; their straight bills go straight down the worm's perpendicular shaft. But the curlew's curved bill cannot do this, and yet he almost invariably captures his worm. Perhaps the problem could be solved by a study of the worm's habits.

To see the curlew feeding in this way you will have to expend much time and patience, for he spends most of his day either resting, or picking up small shellfish or shrimp-like creatures from the surface of the mud or from the bottom of pools.

Away out at the very edge of the sea you may chance upon the little sanderling. It is very similar in size and form to the dunlin, but its upper parts are much paler, freely speckled with white, and there is a broad white band across the wings which is very conspicuous in flight.

The sanderling lives chiefly on sandhoppers and other small creatures which it finds either in or near the wash of the surf, in and out of which it paddles quite unconcernedly even when a larger wave than usual threatens to sweep it off its feet. When it changes ground it usually proceeds in a curving flight a few yards out over the sea. As a rule it feeds in small scattered parties, but sometimes consorts with flocks of dunlin.

The knot is also similar to the dunlin, but is larger, more heavily built and shorter in the leg. It lives here as a rule in large flocks, the members of which always keep close together even when they are feeding. In its summer dress, which you may see in spring before the flocks set out for their nesting ground in the far north, the breast has a rosy tinge.

Feeding among the wrack at high-water mark or on stony parts of the beach, you may see the turnstone, one of the most interesting of all the waders. This bird, which belongs to the plover branch of the family, has the clever trick of thrusting his bill under a stone and heaving it over in order to capture any small creature that may be hiding under it. When I have been watching him I have been surprised at the large size of the stones he is able to turn. If the weight proves too much for his bill alone, he raises it so far, then presses his breast against it and so pushes it over.

Large and conspicuous among the inhabitants of the mudflats stands out the shelduck, whose bold black and white plumage is visible at a great distance, whether he is feeding, swimming or flying. The beautiful broad chestnut band on his breast and his bright red bill and feet are only noticeable at close quarters, except with the aid of field glasses.

This species is more than a duck and not quite a goose. It forms a link between these two branches of the family.

Offshore in similar localities and in the same seasons, you may see many species of diving birds. The cormorant will be there, but there may also be several kinds of duck, some of which you will never see on lakes, two or more grebes, and one or more divers.

In certain circumstances every species of duck visits the ocean. Flocks of mallard which feed at night on lakes near the coast, almost invariably seek refuge at dawn in estuaries or in the open sea. Widgeon may often be seen in considerable numbers on inland lakes, but their favourite food is a kind of grass called *zostera marina* (but which might be better known if it were named widgeon grass), which grows just below high-water on muddy or sandy shores. Where there is a large bed of this plant, flocks of widgeon may be looked for when the tide begins to ebb.

The scaup duck is an occasional visitor to inland lakes, but it is a true sea duck and feeds chiefly on mussels. It might obtain these on the foreshore at low tide, but is an expert diver and so can feed in greater safety and over a longer period while the tide is both ebbing and flowing. The drake has a silvery back and a dark green head and neck. As mussels do not live in very deep water, the scaup may be watched at work from the shore, and at such times the flock is always extended in a scattered line.

In deeper parts live the scoter and the velvet scoter, both of which are large black ducks, the latter distinguished by a conspicuous white patch on the wings. There also you may see the long-tailed duck, which must not be confused with the pintail which visits our inland lakes, and the wonderful eider duck which lives chiefly on razor-shellfish and secures them by diving in water up to about fifty feet in depth.

The red-breasted merganser is another common winter visitor to our estuaries. He is a very handsome diving duck with a dark green head and neck, and a bright chestnut breast. You will know him from the other ducks by the fact that his bill, instead of being broad and flat, is narrow and tapering, and at first sight gives him more the appearance of a grebe than a duck. Like the grebes and cormorants he preys on fish and pursues them under water, so you must not expect him to rise again where he dives.

Many great crested grebe leave their summer quarters on our reedy lakes and spend the winter fishing in our estuaries. Thither also resort for food and shelter the Slavonian, the black-necked and the red-necked grebe. They are smaller than the great crested, and are very much alike in form and bearing, but of course each has his own special characteristics. Their identification calls for keen and quick eyesight and a clever use of field glasses, and they are so active and, when fishing, so intent on their work that they are a constant delight to watch.

Still more aquatic in their habits, and, if possible, more skilful in diving and swimming, are the birds which have been specially honoured with the name of diver. In summer the red-throated and the black-throated divers nest on the banks of lochs in Scotland, but in winter they confine themselves to the sea. In their winter plumage they are not easily distinguished from each other, or from the great-northern diver which visits our coasts at this season. The general colouring of all three is dark brown, but the back of the commonest, namely, the red-throated diver, is freely speckled with white. Similar markings in grey on the other two are not conspicuous. Of these species the commoner is the great-northern diver.

The divers are larger than the grebes, and are distinguished from the ducks by their sharp-pointed beaks.

While you are watching the birds of the shore and the sea, you may have the good fortune to spy a seal either resting on a rock or swimming near the margin. This will most probably be the common seal, which has a round head and looks startlingly like a man swimming with the breast stroke. The common seal dives frequently, and after an interval of several minutes, comes up again some distance from the spot where he disappeared.

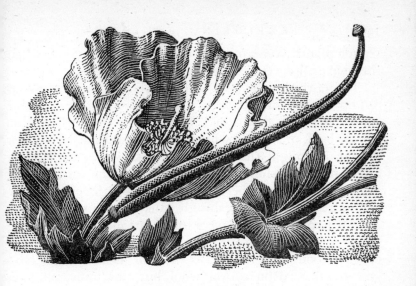

CHAPTER TEN

THE COAST — SEASIDE FLOWERS

AT the seaside you will see many plants which you may know well elsewhere, but there will be many others which may be new to you and which are to be found only on or near the seashore. The seaweeds, which must be covered by salt water for some part of their lives, stop at high-water mark, but land plants advance across the sand or shingle almost to the wash of the waves.

The handsomest of all these seashore flowers is the yellow horned poppy. When you see it in bloom you cannot help knowing that it is a cousin of the common poppy, though its large silky petals are yellow instead of red. But you would hardly recognise the family likeness in the rest of the plant. Its stem and leaves are thick and fleshy, and are covered with a peculiar bluish-grey, or, as it is usually called, glaucous skin. You will notice that many other seaside plants have similar features, so you may guess that they have all developed them for similar reasons.

The horned poppy is a solitary plant which grows far out on the sand or shingle where very few other land plants could exist. The first time I found it, it was flourishing on a wide bank of shingle where there was no sign of sand or soil, so I thought that its roots must reach some kind of earth under the stones, and I began to search for it. But I removed a great number of stones and still there were more and more (for, of course, shingle banks are many feet thick), and all I could discover were long, thread-like roots going down and down between them. Plants, however, get most of their food from the air, as those of us know who have grown mustard on cotton wool, but they must all have water, and those that live in soil are able to take it as they want it from the damp earth. They draw it up through their stems and breathe it out as vapour through their leaves.

When rain falls on shingle it quickly trickles down between the stones and disappears. The roots of the horned poppy catch and suck up some of it as it passes, but if the plant then allowed this to evaporate through its leaves, it might die of thirst before the next shower fell. So instead, it grows those thick stems and leaves and stores the liquid in their cells. Very little evaporates, and thus it is able to live for a long time in dry weather without drinking. In this respect it resembles the camel, which swallows enough water to last it for several days when it is crossing the desert.

But the most remarkable feature of this poppy is its horn. There is no sign of this till after the flower has withered, but then it grows up quickly and is soon six inches or a foot in length. It is really a pod and contains the seeds.

There is sure to be a cornfield not far off with the common poppy growing in it. So you should compare the two kinds. The common poppy does not have pods; it grows its seeds in a round or oval box with a number of different compartments, each with a little window at the top through which it throws them when they are ripe.

The sea rocket is another common plant which grows on the sand quite close to the sea. It has thick fleshy stems and leaves of the same glaucous colour as those of the horned poppy. The stems are very crooked, so it is not an attractive plant except when it is in bloom, and then it is beautiful. Its flowers are usually lilac but sometimes white, and they have four petals arranged in the form of a cross. It has a peculiar pod which is divided into two sections by a joint. Each section contains only one seed. The upper one drops off when ripe, but the lower one remains attached to the plant.

All the other members of its family have similar flowers, so they are known as the cross-bearers. It is a very large and important family, and you already know many members of it. If you keep the name in mind you will easily recognise any plants that belong to it by the form of their flowers, and this will be a great help to you when you wish to look up their names in your flower books. The books call it cruciferæ, but that just means cross-bearers.

Some familiar species are stock and wallflower, lady's smock or cuckoo flower, and charlock, the yellow weed that is so common in cornfields. But still more important ones are cabbage, kale, Brussels sprouts, cauliflower, broccoli, and radish. When you think of these plants growing in our comfortable kitchen gardens, it is difficult to imagine that they could ever live on the seashore, yet that is where they all originally came from.

Strange to tell, the wild cabbage flourishes on the ledges of rocky cliffs or among the stony debris at the foot of them. Its leaves are large and spreading, and do not crowd round each other to form the wonderful "heart" which is the important part of its tame cousin. You will more easily recognise it when you think of a cultivated cabbage that has been allowed to run to seed.

Those of our forefathers who lived on the coast discovered this plant and found that it was good to eat. So they planted it in their gardens and there it became the mother of the common garden cabbage, and also of kale, Brussels sprouts, cauliflower and broccoli.

You will find the wild cabbage only on the south and western coasts of England. The fisher folk in some places still eat its leaves in winter.

The wild radish is a common weed of our cornfields, but both this and the radish of our kitchen gardens originally came from the seashore, and there you will find direct descendants of the founder of the family still growing. You will be able to identify this plant best by its pods, which are divided by several joints and have a long beak on the tip.

Beetroot and mangold wurzel are descended from a common ancestor which lived on the seashore, and the savage tribe to which it belonged is still to be found there. The wild beet is one of those weeds which most of us pass by as not worth notice as it does not have beautiful blossoms. It belongs to quite a different family from the cabbage. Its flowers are small and green, and large numbers of them are grown close together on tall spikes. Though this plant is so unattractive in appearance, it is, nevertheless, one of the most interesting in the world, because it has provided us not only with a vegetable for ourselves and another for our cattle, but also with most of our sugar, which is now obtained from white beetroot. You will find it growing on muddy parts of the shore, and especially in brackish ditches.

Two seaside plants which are much more attractive because of their conspicuous flowers, are the sea campion and the sea convolvulus, or bindweed. You might easily pass by the sea campion, thinking that it was just the common bladder campion which you see so plentifully on the roadsides and in the fields at home. You should notice, however, that it produces its blossoms singly as a rule, and not in pairs or little bunches as the common bladder campion does. Its leaves, too, are rounder and thicker than those of the inland species.

The sea convolvulus has pale pink blossoms, which are almost as large as the white bells of the greater bindweed which climbs on the hedgerows. Its stems, however, are short and are more inclined to trail on the ground than to climb. The two common bindweeds, the lesser and the greater, have sharp-pointed spear-like leaves, but the leaves of the sea convolvulus have short rounded tips and so are somewhat kidney-shaped.

The sea campion and the sea convolvulus are both cousins of similar inland species. On the other hand, the sea holly is not in any way related to the true holly. It has been so named because of its prickly leaves which resemble the familiar foliage of the holly tree. When you see its beautiful blue flower heads you might think that it was some kind of thistle. Examine them carefully, however, and you will discover that each floret sits in its own separate bracket. Each of them ought to have a little stalk, for the head is really an umbrella which has lost its spokes. The plant, therefore, belongs to the same family as hemlock, hedge parsley, wild carrot, and so on. You should compare one of the heads with a thistle head and note the difference between the two. You will notice that the petals of the sea holly florets have long points which are turned down inwards. Sea holly is very common on sandy shores.

On rocky shores and cliffs you will find the beautiful sea pink. At first sight this looks as if it might be cousin to the cornflower, which, of course, is related to the thistle. Each floret on the head of a sea pink, however, has a little stalk of its own. The head grows up on a tall, thin, wiry stem, from the midst of a bunch of long, narrow, stiff leaves.

There is a little mystery in the life of the sea pink. It grows abundantly on the shore and on the face and edge of cliffs, but only a few yards away you will see no sign of it. That, of course, is true of most seaside plants. Many miles away, however, and high up among the rocks of the mountain tops you will find the sea pink again. The question is, how did it get there

When its seeds are ripe they are carried away by the wind on a light, five-winged parachute. It is possible that some of them may have been borne all those miles and dropped on the mountain tops, but not likely. No doubt many of the seeds are eaten by hungry birds when they arrive on our shores after their long journey from their winter quarters. Some of these seeds may be swallowed whole and dropped undamaged many hours later when the birds are crossing the mountains, and, finding among the barren rocks similar conditions to those of their seashore home, they germinate and flourish. Or perhaps the sea pink grew among those rocks before the mountains were raised and has lived there ever since. At any rate, if you ever meet with the mountain sea pink you will notice that its leaves are rather broader than those of the shore sea pink.

On the forbidding salt marshes you will find two very

It grows abundantly on the shore and on the face and edge of cliffs.

beautiful flowers, sea lavender and sea aster. Sometimes they are in such quantities that they look almost as if they had been planted for market, and make a wonderful display of colour.

The sea lavender is not related to the true lavender, but **is** a cousin of the sea pink and has been given its name from the colour of its flowers. Instead of being grouped in little globes like those of the sea pink, they are placed in rows along one side of the stalk, which bends over at the tip so that they may all look up at the sky.

There are two forms of the sea aster. One has a yellowish centre surrounded by mauve rays which give it very much the appearance of the Michaelmas daisy. The other has the yellow centre without the rays or with only a very few.

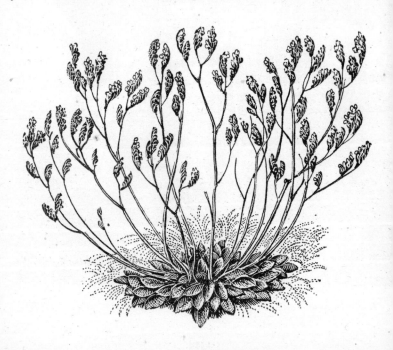

CHAPTER ELEVEN

WHEN THE TIDE IS OUT

WHEN the tide is out, the foreshore is a more or less narrow strip of ground on which the conditions of life for its various inhabitants would seem to be the same everywhere. Of course, in some parts it is rocky and in some sandy, and wherever it is one or the other, we may expect to find creatures peculiar to that environment. But whether it is sandy or rocky, or both, it is, as a whole, divided into three spheres by invisible lines. These are the part near high tide, the part about half tide and the part at low tide. It is useful to remember these divisions when you go hunting on the shore, because while some of its denizens may be found in all three, each has a special population of its own. This knowledge helps you to identify many of your trophies, or enables you to go in search of particular species with a reasonable certainty of finding them, just as you would know where to look for a corn marigold, or the anemone or heather.

For example, near high-water mark the seaweeds are mostly green. Between that point and half tide they are brown, and in deep water at and beyond low tide they are red. There is an obvious exception to this rule. Just below low tide you will see a forest of long ribbon-like weeds waving about in the water. Some have square edges and tops, others have crinkled edges and pointed tips. Among them you will also find the curious whipcord weed which may be twenty or thirty feet long. All these are brown, and the explanation is that they are tall enough to obtain as much light as those that live farther inshore. The rare red weeds, which are sometimes thrown up after a storm, are short, and as they grow at the bottom of deep water they obtain very little light. The green weeds in the shallow water near high-water mark receive almost as much sunlight as the land plants.

The commonest of the brown weeds are the wracks of which there are four species. Of these, the best known are the bladder wrack and the whistle wrack. The bladder wrack has heart-shaped fruits at the tips of its fronds, and small bladders in pairs filled with air lower down which support them in the water. The knobbed or whistle wrack has large bladders on narrower fronds, and is so named because the bladders when dry may be made into whistles. They are often also converted into very efficient squirts by boys while they are still fresh. The other two wracks have no bladders. One, the serrated wrack, may be recognised by the toothed edges of its fronds, the fourth by a furrow which runs down the middle of its stem. This last is much more limited in its range than the others, and is only to be found near high-water mark.

In the pools about half tide you may see several more brightly coloured weeds. There is one of a wonderful violet tint, and another of a rich crimson which grows in the shade of overhanging rocks. There is also the peacock weed which is striped horizontally with various shades of green, orange and red. At low tide you may find in the pools the beautiful pink braided hair weed.

Like the daisy on dry land, the sea-snail is to be found on all parts of the foreshore wherever there are weed-covered rocks. It feeds upon sea weeds, and does so by rasping them with a tiny file armed with hundreds of minute teeth. By his means it scrapes off parts of the surface of the leaves and then swallows them. You may come upon snails of several colours, brown, yellow, black or green. These are not different species, but just variations of one species.

You may find any number of whelk shells at or above high-water mark, but you are not likely to meet with the live animal anywhere on the foreshore. This creature lives in the deep water beyond low tide. The empty shells of whelks' eggs are also common on the shore in summer. A great many of them are packed close together in a round bunch about the size of a tennis ball, and they are so light when they are dry that the wind bowls them merrily along the level sand. At first it is difficult to believe that this ball of eggs could have been laid by a whelk, for taken as a whole it is larger than the creature itself. When they were laid, however, they were quite tiny, but their shells were absorbent and elastic. So very soon they began to drink in sea water, and as they did so they expanded gradually till, when the young whelks were ready to be hatched, they had reached the size at which we know them. The young break their way through the shells in spring, and sometimes at that season you may find the egg-balls on the sands still

quite whole, having been dragged from their moorings b
a storm.

The dog whelk, which is a much smaller animal, is ver
common on the rocks and in the pools at low tide. You ma
recognise it by the rows of tiny knobs which run from it
peak to its base. The main colouring of its shell is brownish
In the same sphere you will find the periwinkle and th
sting winkle. The latter, in spite of its name, really belong
to the whelk family. Its shell is whitish, and has a numbe
of crinkled ridges running round it and also from top t
bottom.

The dog periwinkle is an inhabitant of the half tid
sphere. Its shell is blue black.

A very interesting shellfish of the low tide area is th
purpura. It has a white shell marked with orange rings, sc
its name does not describe its appearance. It is derived from
the fact that the animal secretes a substance which, whe
exposed to the air, passes through various colours and
eventually becomes purple. It was from this substance tha
the purple dye so highly esteemed in ancient times wa
obtained.

All these animals have spiral shells. The cowrie and th
limpet are examples of other types of single-shelled molluscs
The cowrie shell is oval and shallow, and has a rounded to
somewhat like a tinker's tent. The limpet's is peaked an
resembles a tiny bell tent.

The limpet is so common and apparently so unenterpris
ing that we are apt to pass it by with only a casual glance
But whenever you come upon a colony of this animal it
will be worth your while to examine it carefully, for there
are several different kinds of limpet. The common limpe
has no opening in its shell which, when the tide is out, it
holds down so firmly that it might almost be a part of the

ock. You could lift it only by the exercise of very great
orce, but if you were to take it unawares with a sudden
harp, sidelong blow you could knock it off quite easily.
This is actually done by that very handsome bird of the
eashore, the oyster-catcher or sea pie. There is also the
eyhole limpet which has an aperture in the tip of its shell
haped like a keyhole, and the fissure limpet which has a
narrow opening in one side which at once suggests the
loorway of a bell tent. Through these holes the animals
nhale and expel water, but they are obviously a weakness
n the armour and may account for the comparative rarity
of their owners. But even the common limpet is not free
rom attack through its shell. You may often pick up a
impet shell with a neat round hole pierced in it. This is
he work of the dog whelk or the sting winkle which are
arnivorous and prey upon other shellfish, boring their
vay in with their file-like tongues and then cutting the
lesh to pieces with the same instrument.

On the sandy shores the conditions are different, and
onsequently you will find there another type of shellfish.
This has two shells instead of only one. Common species
re the cockle, the gaper and the razor shell. It is easy to
ind heaps of their empty shells at high-water mark, but
vhen the tide is out the living animals are not be to seen
nywhere. There are actually thousands of them, but they
re hidden in the sand. But though they are out of sight,
hey cannot help betraying their presence. Wherever you
o, from about half tide onwards, you will see little jets of
vater spouting out of the sands like tiny springs. But the
low of a spring is continuous, and these are intermittent.
Under each there is a bivalve shellfish which breathes by
lrawing water in through one of two tubes and squirting
t out through the other. It would seem a simple matter

to dig them up, but it is useless to try except to prove wha
I say, for the shellfish can burrow much more quickly tha
you can dig. But it is easy to catch them where the sand i
soft enough to enable you to thrust your hand down int
it quickly as deep as the elbow. You can do this at the edg
of a pool, and it is worth while bringing the shellfish to th
surface if only to see for yourself how quickly it can di
appear. It thrusts out a curious foot and digs its way int
the sand so rapidly that you are left wondering whether yo
dreamt that you caught it.

This foot is used for another purpose. When the tide i
in, the shellfish come from their burrows and move abou
and they do so by leaping with their single foot. So powe
ful is this organ that a cockle can leap five or six feet at
time. Sometimes cockles come out and jump across the w
sand to meet the incoming tide.

If you cannot catch a cockle or a gaper with your hand
go out to low tide and where you see a shellfish spout, dro
a little salt. In a few moments a razor shell will come t
the surface. It seems incredible that a creature that lives i
salt water should object to salt, but it does. This creatur
will give you a more spectacular demonstration of it
burrowing powers than the others, because its foot is a
one end of its long shell and so it must raise itself uprigh
before it can complete its boring operations.

The scallop, whose shells are very common on sand
shores, lives beyond low tide. It moves about freely, bu
not by jumping. Instead, it swims by opening and closin
its shells.

The mussel is a bivalve which prefers a rocky shore.
attaches itself to stones or rocks or piers by means of
bunch of very tough hairs, and at first sight would seem t
be as unenterprising as the limpet. But it is capable o

moving from point to point by taking a fresh hold with some of its hairs, then letting go with the others and drawing itself forward.

In the rock pools you may find several kinds of anemone. The commonest of them is the beadlet, which varies in colour from green to red. You may see it attached to rocks which have been left high and dry and then it looks just like a little lump of jelly, but when it is covered by water it opens its mouth and spreads its tentacles, and then it looks like a wonderful flower of the daisy family. Indeed, I think that sea daisy would be a better name for these wonderful creatures than sea anemone. When it is fully expanded you will see among the outer tentacles a ring of bright blue knobs like turquoise beads. It is from these that the creature obtains its name.

Right out at low tide you will find in the rock pools the most beautiful of all our anemones. It is called the dahlia, and that name will help you to identify it. Its tentacles are short and thick and are brilliantly banded with red and white. Its disc varies very much in colour and may be red, green, purple or orange. When its tentacles are spread it may be five or six or even more inches in diameter. Nevertheless if you wish to see it you will have to search for it. You might fail to see it though it were right before your eyes, for it has a habit of covering itself with pebbles and other debris.

Though they look as if they grew upon the rocks, anemones are capable of moving from one place to another if they wish. One species has found a ready means of transport by attaching itself to the shell of a hermit crab. The two creatures thus form a kind of partnership, for the anemone is not a parasite. In return for the service it derives from the crab, it destroys large numbers of minute

creatures which might be very troublesome to the crab i
they got into its shell. For the hermit has a soft body un
protected by the usual hard skin of the crab family. Tha
is why it takes possession of the empty shells of molluscs
The body is so soft that the creature is able to curl it roun
inside the spiral shell and so take such a firm grip that it i
impossible to draw it from its den without seriously harm
ing it. Unlike the shellfish, the hermit crab is not confine
to one shell all its life. In its earlier stages it utilises th
empty shell of one of the smaller molluscs such as th
periwinkle or dog whelk, but all its life it is a confirme
househunter, and often seems to change shells for the mer
sake of the change.

Starfish and sea urchins are common inhabitants of th
rock pools. Unlike though they may seem, they are ver
closely related. The sea urchin is really a starfish with it
rays turned up and over till their tips meet. If you examin
the empty shell of a sea urchin you will be able to trace th
five rays quite easily. You will also notice in the shell
large number of tiny pin holes. Through each of these th
creature was able to protrude at will a little sucker by whicl
it could attach itself to rocks or stones and draw itself along
or even climb at quite a remarkable pace. The starfish ha
no shell, but in the groove on the underside of each ray i
has similar suckers, which it can thrust forth from it
tough skin when it wishes to travel.

Besides the hermit crab and the shore or green crab an
the edible crab, there are several others which you may fin
on our shores. For example, there is the spider crab whicl
has a very small body and very long legs, the thorny cral
which has sharp points all over its back, and has a habit o
covering itself with seaweed or other materials so that i
may resemble its environment, the masked crab, which ha

markings on its back resembling a human face, and the pea crab, which is so small that it can live inside the shell of a living mussel.

The lobster family is also a large one. Besides the common lobster, which lives in the deep sea, it includes the shrimp, the prawn and the sandhopper. You may see the shrimps and the prawns darting about in the pools, but as they are almost transparent you will have to catch them in a net if you wish to examine their forms. Like the lobster their bodies are flexible, and they swim by suddenly jerking the tail downwards. The effect of this is that they dart backwards at a great pace.

The sandhopper is very common at high-water mark. If you catch one and place it on your open hand, you will see that it leaps by first doubling its body and then suddenly straightening it like a released spring.

CHAPTER TWELVE

GARDEN, FARM AND TOWN

WE cannot help knowing the common sparrow, for wherever we make our home, whether in city, town, village or open country, there he makes his too. He is so common and familiar that we are apt to pass him by as of no consequence. But look at his plumage. The cock sparrow has a different colour scheme from the hen. You may know him to be the cock by his black bib and his grey head with a chestnut band on each side and at the back of the neck. But even so his plumage is not always the same. In winter it is duller than it is in summer, and this is specially noticeable on the bib, which in winter is much broken up with white, but in spring becomes solid black. This change, however, is not brought about by a moult in spring. Like all other birds he moults in August and puts on his new winter suit. This is the same as his summer suit except that many of the feathers are tipped with either white or buff. These white and buff tips wear away gradually owing to the action of wind and weather, and by the end of February the whole plumage is brightened and the bib has been enlarged and has become one continuous patch of black.

When the young sparrows have left the nest, you will notice that they are all alike and that their plumage is similar to that of their mother. Their colours, however, are paler, so it is easy to distinguish them from the old hens. The young of many other species also resemble the mother, but not all as I will show presently.

The sparrow builds a very untidy nest as everybody knows, but it is a very remarkable structure nevertheless. Usually it is placed under the eaves of a house, hence the name house-sparrow, but occasionally a pair select a site among the branches of a tree. When this happens you will see the primeval nest of the common sparrow. It is a large untidy ball of straw with no obvious entrance. The bird enters and leaves her home through the side, as a harvest mouse does. When, however, the nest is built under cover, the bird seems to understand that an artificial roof is unnecessary. At any rate she omits the dome, and contents herself with a loose pile of straw, in the centre of which she makes a little cup which she lines with feathers. In farmyards large numbers of sparrows nest in the hay and corn stacks and they they do not trouble to collect material, but press down a little round bed with their bodies and add the feather lining.

The tree-sparrow is not common everywhere. He is not to be found at all in cities and towns, but he is fairly common in some suburban districts, and he frequently consorts with the flock of common sparrows that inhabit a farmyard. You will recognise him by the fact that his head is chestnut, not grey, and his cheek is white with a large black spot in the middle of it. The cock and the hen tree-sparrow are alike. In spite of its name this species does not build its nest on the branches of trees, but always in a hole, which may be in a tree but may also be in the roof of an old building or elsewhere.

The robin is a good example of a bird whose young are not coloured like the mother. The cock and the hen robins are both brown with a brick red breast, but the young are buff, speckled all over with brown. This plumage is very similar to that of young thrushes, blackbirds, nightingales, and certain others, and, as these species are all related, it is believed that they are descended from a common ancestor which was so coloured, and that this juvenile dress is a relic and a record of those far off days.

In August the young robin discards his speckled plumage and replaces it with a complete new suit in full adult colours. About this time he begins to make his first experiment in singing, and he goes on practising till, about the beginning of October, he has become as good a performer as his father. Then the air is full of the singing of robins, and the whole countryside astir with their quarrelling.

This fighting is surprising and significant because it is just the opposite of what happens among other birds. At the approach of autumn they sink all their jealousies and gather in flocks so that they may face the trials and dangers of winter in company. But the robin believes in the principle, "every bird for himself." The birds that flock move about the country in search of food, but the robin settles down in winter quarters in October and remains there till pairing time next spring. But when he has selected his territory he has to prove his right to it, and he can do that only by defending his boundaries by force.

Sometimes this fighting is so fierce that one of the combatants is killed, but in most instances it does not become more serious than skirmishing, and gradually it subsides, each robin having established his sovereignty over a sufficient number of square yards to provide food for himself till nesting time comes round again. But partly to while away the time and partly to remind his neighbours that he is alive and alert, he sings all day long with necessary intervals for feeding.

When spring approaches there is another scramble for territory. Many of the robins that concentrated for the winter in suburbs and round human dwellings move out into the open country, and each cock seizes sufficient land to support himself and his wife and a family of hungry youngsters.

The starling has established himself as a bird of the garden, the village, the town and the city. He nests in holes either in trees or under the eaves, he roosts in hordes on city churches as well as in woods and reed beds, he feeds very energetically on lawns and fields, doing a vast amount of good by destroying enormous numbers of grubs, and all the year round he makes heroic attempts to sing from the chimney pots.

When the young starlings leave the nest they are brown, but when they moult in August they put on their full adult dress. This is first glossy purple-black very freely speckled with white or buff, and if you can compare several birds, you may distinguish the younger ones from their elders by the fact that their white spots are the larger. At the same time you will notice that both young and old have brown bills. In January the bill begins to change colour, and before long it is bright yellow. Meanwhile, the white tips of the feathers have been wearing away, and when nesting time

arrives the old birds are resplendent in their spring dress of
black shot with purple and green. The younger birds having
had more white to lose are still slightly speckled.

When they are not actually nesting, starlings feed and
roost in flocks, and their evening games before they finally
retire to rest are one of the wonders of the countryside.
They arrive at the roosting place in bands of various sizes,
and when the whole flock is gathered together, they rise in
the air and wheel and circle above the trees again and again,
each turn being made with the perfection and precision of
a company of guards, as if it were done at the word of
command.

The swallow and the martin have also attached themselves to man, so much so that the latter is usually called
the house martin, and the former used to be known as the
barn swallow. These names are appropriate, because the
martin builds its nest of mud against the side of a house
under the eaves, and the swallow makes a round cup of mud
which it places on a ledge or a rafter which it finds con-
veniently in a barn.

There are various means of distinguishing the two birds,
but the simplest method is to watch them as they turn in
flight and then note the colouring of the back. If there is
a white patch on the rump, that is the lower part of the
back next the tail, the bird is a house martin. If there is no
white on the back, it is probably a swallow; but it may be
a sand martin. The swallow's back, however, is blue-black,
and the sand martin's mouse-brown. The sand martin nests
in holes which it mines for itself in the sides of sand pits
and sandy cliffs, but all three species may often be seen
together hawking for insects over a lake or a stream, and
then the features I have described are invaluable guides to
identification.

The swift used to be classed as one of the swallow tribe. Now, however, we know that it belongs to an entirely different family, but owing to the similarity of its habits to those of the swallow it has developed a somewhat similar form. It is easily recognised by its larger size, its dark brown plumage, its long sickle-like wings and its very short forked tail. It spends all day on the wing, often at a great height, and seems never to tire. It never perches, but sometimes clings for a few seconds to the side of a house, and if it falls to the ground, as I have more than once seen it do after a fight with a starling which had usurped its nesting hole under the eaves, it cannot rise again without assistance.

All our birds fly by lowering and raising both wings at the same time. The swift flies this way also, but very frequently, and always when he is going at top speed, he plies his wings alternately. Many people refuse to believe this and there is little wonder, for his movements are so rapid that the human eye can hardly separate them, but it becomes quite obvious when you compare his manner of flight with that of the swallow or the martin, one of which is very often in the air at the same time.

Like the starlings, the swifts have a game which they play regularly with the wildest enjoyment at the end of the day. Instead, however, of being an exercise of skill in manoeuvring as a flock, it is a trial of speed, endurance and skill in the individual. All the members of a colony take part in it, but one volunteers to be hare and the others accept the challenge and set off in pursuit of him. They turn and wheel, swoop and rise, plunge and dash helter skelter round the house, screaming joyously with excitement like a lot of children, then mount high in the air and proceed as before. If the hare is overtaken one of the others sets off in his place, and so the game goes on.

The swifts are among the latest of our summer visitors to arrive, and among the first to go. In the south of England they appear about the first of May, and most of them leave about the middle of August. So they do not have much time for their nesting, and, as the young birds remain in the nest for about a month, they must have only a few days in which to stretch their wings before they start on their long flight to their winter quarters. So the evening game must be invaluable practice for them.

Swallow and swift live upon insects which they capture on the wing by hawking. The pied wagtail and the fly-catcher are also insect eaters, but each hunts according to a method of his own. The pied wagtail is one of the very few small birds that are able to run. The vast majority hop, but the wagtail has not time to be so leisurely. He may spy a succulent morsel six or eight feet away, and he must reach it if possible before it takes to flight. So he runs, and he is so quick and nimble that he usually succeeds. But if the insect does try to escape he makes a rapid dart into the air and seizes it, then returns to the ground and runs hither and thither again in search of more. At nesting time I have seen a pied wagtail repeatedly hovering over a cornfield till it had collected a mouthful of insects, then flying off to the nest and returning a minute of two later to do the same again. In winter he pays frequent visits to roofs, where he seems to find a good supply of food, and his call note *chisick* or *chirrick* is then very noticeable. At this season he wears white on his throat and a black crescent on his breast, but in spring he replaces this with a complete gorget of black.

The spotted flycatcher has yet another method of hunting. He sits on a branch or fence and waits for an insect to come within his range, then he launches himself into the

*Swallow and swift live upon insects which they capture on the wing
by hawking.*

air, swoops down on the unlucky adventurer, seizes it with an audible snap and returns to his perch.

As rooks nest so early, their operations are not obscured by foliage, so it is easy to watch their methods of building. These birds always winter in a wood at some distance from the rookery, which is usually deserted from June till March. Occasionally, on mild days in January or February, you may see a few pairs inspecting the old nests, but the flock does not definitely enter into possession again till about the first week in March.

Then all is bustle and noise, for the chief business of the year has begun. The old nests are cleaned out, pulled together and repaired, a new stick being inserted here and there to make good the ravages of the winter storms, and a rootlet or two woven in to improve the lining. But what is still more interesting, from the point of view of the watcher, is the building of a nest from the foundations by a new pair. The first few sticks of the structure are sappy twigs which are wrenched from a tree by the rook, and then intertwined with the branches of the fork which has been selected for the site of the nest. A firm platform is thus fabricated, and on it the superstructure is raised with sticks either obtained in the same way or fetched from the ground some distance off; for even if a rook drops a stick in the vicinity of the rookery he will not retrieve it but will go in search of another.

When the eggs are laid and the hens begin to brood, the cock has to work for two. He flies off to the fields and feeds. When he is satisfied he goes on picking up more, but now, instead of swallowing his tit-bits, he stores them in a pouch under his tongue. Having completed his load, he flies back to the rookery, and as he passes overhead you may see under his bill a large lump, which is really the pouch distended with stores for the wife who is patiently sitting on her eggs and waiting for his return.

But when he reaches the home tree he does not go straight to the nest and hand over the treasure, and if you watch there you will see an amusing little domestic drama. He alights on a neighbouring branch and answers his wife's inquiries and demands with apparent indifference, and seems to pretend that he has brought home nothing, though obviously she can see his bulging market basket. At any rate, not until she leaves the nest and treats him to a good deal of wheedling does he consent to hand over the spoil.

The jackdaw may often be seen feeding in the fields with the rook or even flying in company with it. He is a smaller bird, but may be easily recognised by various signs. One is the silver grey patch on the back of his head and neck, another his shorter and less bulky bill which has no bare white patch at its base. When your eye becomes familiar with both birds in flight, you may distinguish the jackdaw by his quicker and shorter wingbeats. But the surest signs of all are his calls, especially the light, sharp note which suggests the name Jack, or might be represented as *kya*.

The most natural nesting site of the jackdaw is a hole high up in the side of a cliff, but he has found that the unglazed lights of a church steeple serve his purpose equally well. Indeed, so popular have such positions become with this species that in almost every town, with the exception of London, a flock of jackdaws has occupied the tower of at least one church for many generations. At nesting time, however, the narrow openings are a great trial to the birds, which usually carry sticks by the middle, and are frequently forced to drop them after bringing them to the very threshold of the home, from sheer inability to drag them

through. Like the rook, the jackdaw never attempts t
recover such lost material, but after gossiping about it fo
a while, he goes off to fetch another. Consequently, for :
week or two in spring, the unlucky sexton is kept constantl
busy sweeping up a litter of sticks from the precincts.

By its very name you know that the barn owl is :
frequenter of buildings. Besides barns it inhabits belfrie
and ruins and sometimes holes in trees. As a rule it hunt
after dark and sleeps during the day, but often in winte
and early spring I have watched it at work in broad day
light. This must mean that there is then a scarcity of suit
able food, that is, of mice, voles and young rats, an
consequently the owl has to do overtime in order to mak
a living. Because it destroys so many of these pests this ow
ought to be protected and encouraged, but instead it ha
been persecuted for centuries and is becoming scarcer.

By day the barn owl is very conspicuous, because it
broad face and under parts are white. At a short distanc
that is the only colour you see, but at close quarters yo
will notice that the upper parts are buff. At dusk it has ;
very ghost-like appearance as it flits silently through th
air. Its call is a startling screech and this, combined wit
its mysterious and ghostly appearance at night, may hav
led superstitious people in the past to destroy it. When it i
angry it hisses like a snake, and the young snore loudl
when they are hungry.

Another winged creature with which every one i
familiar is the bat. That is to say, we are familiar with it
appearance as it flits about at dusk, and we know that i
does not as a rule fly by day, but our knowledge of it usuall
ends there. How many of us are there, for example, wh
are aware that there is more than one species of bat? As ;
matter of fact, there are twelve British species.

Another name we give this animal is flittermouse. This is very misleading, because the creature is not in any way related to the mouse. The mouse is a rodent, whereas the bat is an insect-eater.

The wing of the bat is very different from that of a bird. The four fingers of each hand are very much elongated and are arranged somewhat after the manner of the ribs of an umbrella. They are joined by a leather web which extends to the sides and to the hind limbs (but not to the toes) and also to the tail. The thumbs are short and not webbed, and each carries a short hooked claw which is used for clinging and crawling when the bat alights at the mouth of its retreat, or on the support where it intends to sleep. Later it turns round and hangs head downward by its hind feet.

The common bat has been given the beautiful name pipistrelle. It is the smallest British mammal, but another species that is almost as common and about the same size is the long-eared bat. The ears of the latter are held erect when the creature is in flight and are therefore conspicuous, so it is not difficult to distinguish between the two species if you have quick eyes. But there is also a remarkable difference in their habits of feeding. The pipistrelle always captures its prey on the wing, but the long-eared bat is fond of flitting round the branches of trees and bushes and snatching insects from the leaves or flowers.

When a bat catches a large insect such as a moth or a beetle, he makes a pouch with the tail part of his web, pops the victim into that and holds it there till he can take a firmer grip with his mouth and nip off and drop the wings. The action is momentary, but you may see it done if you watch him closely as he goes to and fro on his beat.

This performance is most noticeable in the activities of the noctule, which is our largest bat. The noctule flies high

as a rule, squeaking loudly as it goes, so it is readily recog
nised, and as you will usually see it against the open sky
you will be able to observe its movements easily.

When a young bat is born, it is at first kept under it
mother's wing. But when she goes hunting she has to carr
her offspring with her, for she has no nest in which to la
it. The youngster then creeps out from under her wing and
clings to the fur on the under side of her body by its teet
and claws. You may look out for mother bats carrying thei
young in July.

If you watch regularly the comings and goings of bats
you will notice that their sleeping place in summer i
different from that which they use in winter. Their winte
quarters are not easily discovered because then they hiber
nate, but it is not difficult to trace their summer dormitory
and if you examine this in late autumn you will find tha
they have deserted it. They do not leave the country, bu
retire to some snugger retreat for their long sleep.

The pipistrelle is the least sleepy of all our bats, and you
may see him not uncommonly flitting about in broad day
light during mild weather in the middle of winter. Ii
summer he comes out at dusk and hunts till sunrise.

A garden is fortunate if it is adopted by a toad. Beside
differing from the frog in possessing a dark, dry, wart
skin, the toad is also heavier in build than that creature
His hind legs are short and are not adapted for jumping.

His movements are very sluggish. He may take a few
short, slow steps and then sit still for an hour, so it is eas
to watch his method of feeding. If an insect flies within
his reach it disappears as if by magic. In this one respec
the toad is as quick as lightning. His mouth opens, hi
tongue shoots out and back again, and his jaws close almos
before you realise that anything has happened. Beside

insects, the toad eats slugs and worms, but he will not touch either unless he sees them move.

In so far as he destroys slugs and insects he is a valuable ally in the garden, for the common graden slug is only destructive. A slug is not a snail that has temporarily abandoned its shell, and it is not a lower form of snail that has not yet acquired a shell. It is actually a special type of the same family, and has dispensed with its shell at any rate as a house. Instead, it has an interior shell or shield which is hidden under the skin on the fore part of the back. The position of this shield is indicated by a distinct oval patch.

Many slugs are harmless. The common black slug, for example, feeds for preference on fungi, even on those that are poisonous to ourselves, so in this respect its activities may be said to be beneficial. In dry localities this slug becomes coppery in colour. Other slugs eat lichens, but the common garden slug which is slate grey with black markings on its sides, does a great deal of damage to cabbage and lettuce and to young plants in the flower garden.

Both slugs and snails deposit their eggs underground. The common garden snail lays from fifty to a hundred.

When the young snail hatches it is already provided with a shell. This consists of one whorl and a half, and is reddish. As the animal grows, the shell is enlarged by the addition of new whorls. Growth is slow in the first season, and when winter approaches and the animal prepares to hibernate, it is still small, but when it wakes up in the following spring it eats voraciously and grows very rapidly, and in a few weeks it reaches maturity with a shell of about five whorls. During hibernation and in dry weather it covers the mouth of its shell with a hard, smooth, glue-like substance. As a rule it buries itself in the ground and lies upside down, but sometimes it hides in a hole in a wall or under eaves. If you find one snail in winter you will probably find many, for at this season the species seem to flock like birds. At any rate companies of snails are frequently found hibernating together.

Slugs and snails usually spend their days hiding or resting, and come out at dusk and in the early morning to feed. But damp weather tempts them out even at midday

The shell of the common garden snail is dirty yellow with irregular dark brown markings, and has a dull rough surface. Another species, which is also common in gardens and wherever there are bushes and trees, is the wood snail It has a very beautiful shell which has a short, somewhat flattened spire, is smooth and polished, and is yellow or pink or white, banded with several clean-cut, dark brown stripes

Earthworms are as unattractive in appearance as a creature can well be, but they are invaluable allies both in the garden and in the open fields, because everything they do is beneficial to the ground. They feed upon withered leaves which they drag into their burrows, and on any decaying vegetable matter they may find in the earth. To obtain the latter they swallow the earth as they burrow and when it has passed through their bodies they throw it up on the surface in the form of the well-known castings These castings are washed away by rain, or they dry and are blown about by the wind, and so the particles of which they consist are scattered. But as these little mounds disappear fresh ones take their places, and so in the course of a few years all the earth in the garden is digested by worms. Thus it is broken up into still finer particles and mixed and chemically treated, and finally is turned out on the surface in the best possible condition for the germination of seed.

The worms come out in the evening to fetch home fresh supplies of dead leaves. These they use in the first place to plug the mouths of their mines and to line the main shaft, but later tear them to shreds and devour them. It is not altogether an easy matter to draw the broad sheet of a leaf into a narrow tube. Worms overcome the difficulty and do so not only by the use of muscular force, but also by the exercise of considerable intelligence. If they were to begin with the stalk which would be an easy fit, they would find themselves brought to a standstill when the broad base of the leaf reached the mouth of the burrow. So they begin with the tip, and thus as it disappears into the shaft the blade is gradually rolled up.

In gardens where there are pine trees the worms are faced with another problem. The pine needles are bound together in twos, threes or fives, so if a worm were to take one of a pair by the tip and draw it into the burrow, the other would remain stretched out on the surface and so would prevent the completion of the task. But the worm very wisely begins with the base where the needles are joined, and so takes them down together with perfect ease. The first time I saw a couple of pine needles protruding from a worm hole, I could only think that a human being had inserted them.

Another benefactor in the garden is the earwig. Nobody likes this insect, partly because of its appearance, partly because of its name, and partly because it does a certain amount of damage to flowers. But whatever harm it may do, it pays for many times over by destroying countless numbers of insect eggs, grubs, and slugs and also much waste material dropped by plants.

The mother earwig is one of the few insects that tend their eggs. She lays them in the ground and remains on guard over them till they are hatched, and even till the young are well grown. The young take about two months to reach maturity, and in that time they change their skins four times. After each moult they are pure white except for their eyes which are black, but in about an hour the skin becomes brown again.

Still other beneficial insects are the hoverfly, the lacewing, and the ladybird whose grubs prey upon greenfly. The hoverfly is banded black and yellow like a wasp, and when hovering has a habit of suddenly darting hither or thither a yard or two away. The lacewing has delicate transparent wings which are beautifully veined with bluish green. Its body is green and its eyes are golden or ruby red and so prominent that it is often called golden eyes. The grub has a habit of covering itself with the skins of its victims. It also feeds in a peculiar way, namely, by raising its head and holding the aphis in the air while it sucks the body dry. The grub of the ladybird is like a tiny black lizard. It devours large numbers of greenfly, and when it grows up and becomes the beautiful red-backed beetle which has the unique distinction among beetles of being loved and welcomed by human beings, it carries on the good work.

Some insects of the garden, on the other hand, are only destructive, for example, the familiar and charming white butterfly. The grubs of both the common and the small white butterfly feed upon cabbage, and if they were not warred against by the gardener, would soon destroy a whole crop. If you look under the cabbage leaves, you will find the eggs of these insects which are tiny yellow cones set up on end. Both species have two broods each year, one in spring and the other in summer, and the second brood differs so much from the first that at one time it was thought to be a separate species.

In the rose garden you will find damage of another kind done by an insect, but unless you are very lucky or very patient you will not see the offender. This time, instead of the sap being sucked or the leaves eaten, large pieces are cut out of the leaves and carried away. It is the work of the leaf-cutter bee. You may see this little insect alight, but she cuts so rapidly that, before you realise what has happened, she is flying away with a round piece of leaf-blade about the size of a shilling, or with a more or less oval or rather figure-of-eight piece about double that size.

She carries several of the larger pieces one after another to a burrow she has made in a tree. Here she places them spirally in such a way as to form a little thimble-like bag. This she fills with honey on which she lays an egg, and then she plugs the mouth with several round pieces of leaf, and proceeds to construct another cell on top of it, and so on.

Hosts of other insects infest the garden, and their presence attracts large numbers of spiders. There may be several species of these creatures even in a small patch, but the most notable of them is the common garden spider, the wonderful engineer that constructs the well-known orb web. During the day this spider, which is also called the diadem spider because of the cream-coloured cross she bears on her back, spends most of her time in her den, which is a little way from the web but is connected with the hub by a thread. This thread serves both as a bridge and as a telegraph wire, for the vibrations of the web caused by the struggles of a captured fly are conveyed along it to the sleeper in the den, and she, waking, runs across it to the centre of her snare and then by one of the spokes to the victim. Then having dispatched the insect with her fangs, she wraps it round with a thick coat of silk, releases it from

the snare, and hoists it up to her den where she can make a
meal of it at her leisure.

Such incidents and also various accidents, such as the
falling of a leaf or a twig through the meshes of the net
or the blundering of a bumble bee or a wasp which are strong
enough to escape, damage the web so seriously in the course
of the day, that it is necessary for the spider to renew the
whole fabric every evening. She usually begins work just
after dusk, but it is easy to watch the whole operation with
the aid of a lantern.

The first step is to pass a cable across the space in which
the web is to be hung. This is accomplished by paying out
a thread and allowing its free end to float in the air till it
becomes attached to something on the other side. As soon
as this happens the spider draws the thread taut, adds several
short stays at each end and doubles and trebles it as she
crosses and recrosses. This done, she can complete her work
without the uncertain aid of air currents. She next passes
a second cable across, some distance below the first and
parallel to it. Then between these two she fixes two more
or less upright threads, and thus forms the framework of
the web. About midway between these she places a perpendicular line, and from about the centre of this she carries
the radial threads of the orb to various points on the frame,
working more or less alternately on each side, top and
bottom.

When this is completed, she begins again from the centre
and lays a spiral line in narrow meshes to a radius of about
half an inch, thus strengthening the fabric and at the same
time forming a platform on which she can sit when she is
not resting in her den. A little beyond this area she starts
again, and still working outwards she lays very rapidly
another spiral line, this time in very wide meshes. You may

now think that the web is finished, but this second spiral is only temporary; it is a scaffolding by means of which she will place in position still another thread, which is the last and most important part of the whole structure.

Starting this time from the circumference, she works spirally towards the centre, removing the scaffolding as she proceeds. You will notice that when she has fixed each section of this final thread, she gives it a twang with one of her feet as if she were testing it. This line, however, unlike the rest of the web, is saturated with gum, and the spider's testing jerk causes the fluid to form a series of tiny globules, which are the real business part of the snare. Without them the web would not be effective and many a likely captive would escape, but the moment an insect strikes this thread the gummy gems besmear its legs and wings and so prevent them from being used to break the snare and set their owner free.

CHAPTER THIRTEEN

FARTHER AFIELD

WHEN you have become familiar with the animal and plant
life in your neighbourhood, you will want to go farther
afield if you have the real spirit of the explorer in you. This
you will do as a matter of course at all holiday times, for
no matter where you go then, you will be in new surroundings, where the soil, the climate and the general conditions
under which the wild creatures live are different from those
to which you have been used, and where, therefore, you will
have fresh opportunities for making discoveries. You will
probably decide to spend some of your holidays in moorland
districts, or among the chalk hills, or by the seaside, or
within easy reach of the marshes, so that you may make the
acquaintance of the plants and animals that inhabit them.
But even when you have done all these things and can claim
that you have a wide general knowledge of the natural

history of your country, you will find that there are still many isolated parts which you must visit in order to add to your list of friends some species, perhaps a few, perhaps only one, which for some reason or other have become confined to particular localities.

For example, the blue hare must be sought on moors high up among the mountains. This species is similar to the common hare, but is smaller and has shorter ears and longer legs. In summer his fur is dark grey, but in winter it becomes white and so renders its owner almost invisible against the snow which covers his homeland at that season. While the change is taking place the grey hair mixed with white gives the animal a bluish appearance, hence the name.

Still higher on the mountains, away up on the grey rocky peaks, you must climb if you wish to see the ptarmigan. This bird is a cousin of the grouse, but is smaller and is easily recognised by its plumage, if your eyes are keen enough to pick it out against its natural background. For the ptarmigan is well protected by its colours. It is exceptional among our birds in that it changes its plumage three times a year. In summer the cock is dark brown, but after his autumn moult he becomes grey above and white underneath. This plumage is so like the rocks among which he lives that it is almost impossible to see him then unless he moves. As he lives at such high altitudes, however, even grey would be conspicuous among the snow which lies on the mountain tops all winter and far into spring. So as the year advances he moults again, and this time his new suit is pure white.

In the pine forests of the Spey valley in Scotland, an area of thirty miles long by ten miles broad, lives the little crested tit. This bird is not known in any other part of Britain, but it is found plentifully in pine forests on the continent. How then can this feathered mite have become isolated in that remote northern glen It is believed that the species is a relic of the days when the greater part of Britain was covered with pine forests. As these were gradually destroyed and replaced by other kinds of trees, the natural home of the crested tit became more and more limited, until at length it was reduced to the one large forest in the Spey valley. Since then pines have been planted again in many parts of the country, so in time the crested tit may multiply and spread, but meanwhile you must go to this one locality if you wish to make its acquaintance.

Though it is called the crested tit, you might easily mistake it for the blue tit at first sight by its size and manner and the paleness of its crown, for the crest is raised only when the bird is excited. But when the crest is raised there can be no doubt about the species, for the feathers of its crown, which are black banded with white, are elongated and so stand up on its head very conspicuously.

A similar fate befell many marsh birds when the fens were drained. Their feeding and nesting places vanished, and they were forced to seek new quarters elsewhere or die. Several species which are regular travellers, no longer nest in this country though they visit it frequently, but one little resident, the bearded tit, has remained in dwindling numbers among the reeds on the Norfolk Broads. The way to see this charming little bird is to sit in a boat between two reed beds and wait till it flies across from one to the other. Then you may have a good view of it as it sits for a few moments on the top of a reed. It has a long tail and is very brightly and beautifully coloured, and the male has a tuft of black feathers sticking out on each side of his bill, which have the appearance of a very handsome moustache rather than of a beard.

This species has a very remarkable call note. If you balance a penny on the tip of your finger and then strike its edge lightly with another you will get some idea of the sound which may be described as *ping*, only the bird's note is louder and more explosive. In fact, when it misses fire, as it not infrequently does, the impression you get is that of the shooting of an air-pistol.

I have thought it worth while to pay more than one visit to the Norfolk Broads for the sake of seeing and hearing the bearded tit, but at the same time I have seen and heard other birds which are equally rare.

The bittern used to be common not only in the fens but also in other suitable parts of England, but now it is confined to one or two of the Broads. It is a large bird, and when in flight is similar to the heron only brown instead of grey. As it skulks among the reeds it is seldom seen except when on the wing, but it has a most astonishing mating call which can be heard at a great distance. This can best be described as a kind of cross between the braying of an ass and the honking of a motor horn. The honk is loud and resounding, but at close quarters you can hear the intake of the breath before each blow, and it is this that reminds you of the donkey's bray.

In the same neighbourhood you may see Montague's harrier and the marsh harrier, two large birds of the hawk tribe which hunt across the marshes and nest on the ground there. It is a wonderful sight to watch these great birds floating gracefully low down over the flat wastes on their long, beautifully shaped wings, and a special treat to see the male Montague's harrier feeding his mate when she is brooding.

On sandy wastes and chalk downs in the eastern and southern counties of England you may look for the stone curlew, a large member of the wader family which, though it has long legs well suited for the purpose, has given up wading and prefers to pick up its living on dry ground. You must travel to the far north of Scotland to find the red necked phalarope, which is quite a small member of the same family. Like its large relative, the stone curlew, this bird has also given up wading, but instead of seeking food on waterless sand or chalk, it has taken to swimming, and you will see it sailing about buoyantly on the surface of remote reedy lochs. Another wader which must be sought in most unlikely places is the dotterel, which nests on the tops of the highest mountains in Scotland.

The spotted flycatcher and the pied flycatcher are both summer visitors. Both arrive first on the south coast. The spotted flycatcher then spreads throughout the greater part of England, but for some unknown reason the pied fly-catcher passes over hundreds of miles of tempting sites and wings his way to the valleys in the north of England and Wales.

This handsome little bird differs in several ways from his sober-coated cousin. He is very conspicuous on account of his brilliant black and white plumage, and he sings a very sweet song. As his name shows he feeds on flies, but he is not so clever at the sport of catching them in flight as his cousin, and often he picks them from the ground or snatches them as they rest on the herbage. When he is engaged on this work he frequently returns to one perch, but not as constantly as does the spotted flycatcher.

All our warblers are summer visitors except one, and this one, the Dartford warbler, is rare. He is to be found only on gorsy commons in the south of England, but when you have once identified him you will see him at the same place all the year round.

*The dotterel, which nests on the tops of the highest mountains in
Scotland.*

Formerly the raven was well known in all parts of the country, and then it nested as a rule in tall inaccessible trees. But it did so much mischief that it was gradually driven out of the cultivated districts, and is now only to be found in neighbourhoods where it can nest on rocky sea cliffs or on mountain precipices.

The chough, another member of the crow family, which has always nested on cliffs, is becoming very rare, and is now to be seen only on or near the coast in the south-west of England, in Wales, in the Isle of Man and in some of the western isles of Scotland.

The black-throated and the red-throated divers nest on the banks of small lochs in the Hebrides and the far north of Scotland.

The grey-lag goose also breeds in those remote parts, but large flocks of this and five other species of wild geese visit our coasts regularly every winter. Each species returns year after year to the same neighbourhood, so you must ascertain where their favoured haunts are, and set out one Christmas holiday on a wild goose chase. The domestic goose is a sluggish and stupid creature, but the wild goose is a clever and wary bird and well able to take care of itself. That is why a wild goose chase has become proverbial. But though you may never get near a flock of these birds, you may have the wonderful experience of seeing fifty or a hundred or perhaps a thousand of them flying overhead in long lines or in V formation, and all keeping their places as perfectly as a regiment of soldiers on parade.

A similar story may be told of other forms of animal life, and of plant life. For example, the common toad is found everywhere, but the natterjack toad, a much livelier species, is confined almost exclusively to the fens. The garden snail also is common everywhere, but the still larger edible snail lives only here and there in the south of England, and especially where the ground is chalky. One small species of snail is very plentiful, but only on the chalk downs near the sea in Kent and Sussex.

On the shore near chalk or limestone cliffs, but nowhere else, you may pick up the shells of a bivalve shellfish called the piddock. They are long and narrow and at one end they are studded with teeth. They are thin and brittle, and yet their owner spent its life burrowing in the rock. Britannia would never have ruled the waves but for the ceaseless labours of this strange creature, for by its constant burrowing in the chalk, the sea was enabled gradually to break its way through the strip of land which once joined England to France between Kent and Normandy.

Again, the species of wasp which builds its nest in gooseberry and currant bushes is very common in Scotland and the west of England but rare in the south-east, and the hornet may be found only in the south.

You must go to the fens if you wish to see the beautiful swallowtail butterfly. The common blue butterfly abounds everywhere, but the chalkhill blue, as its name implies, is to be found only in chalk or limestone districts. The Adonis blue is limited to Surrey, Sussex, and Kent, and the large blue to the Cotswolds. Certain species of moth and of other insects are isolated in a similar way in various parts of the country.

Now, the chalkhill blue butterfly lives on the chalk hills for the very good reason that its food plants, the rock rose and the kidney vetch, are confined almost exclusively to such situations. The rock rose is not a rose at all, but its delicate yellow petals give it the appearance of one. On the other hand, the strange plant called the salad burnet, which is another chalk flower, is a real rose, though it has not a single petal by which to show its relationship. Many other plants are to be found only or almost exclusively in chalky or limestone districts. Among them are the horseshoe vetch, which has zig-zag pods, the clustered bell-flower, a very handsome plant with large blue bells grown in a cluster at the top of the stem, the beautiful and wonderful bee orchid whose petals are so coloured as to give the impression that a bee has alighted on them and is sucking the honey, and its two cousins, the fly and the spider orchids, which bear striking likenesses to the creatures after which they are named.

A number of rare plants grow in isolated localities in various parts of the country. For example, every one knows the primrose and the cowslip, for they are common. But the oxlip is limited to a few places in Essex, Suffolk, Bedford and Cambridge. The bird's eye primrose, which has lilac petals with a yellow centre, may be found only in the north of England, and you must go to Caithness, Sutherland or Orkney if you wish to see the Scotch primrose, which has blue petals with yellow at the mouth of the tube. The cinque-foil, the tormentil, the strawberry and the silverweed are common everywhere, but another member of their family, the rock potentilla, is found only in two spots in Wales.

A number of very rare plants are scattered here and there on the mountain tops of Scotland, some on a few peaks and some on only one. At first sight their existence there is a mystery. They are found also in similar situations in Scandinavia, in the Alps and in the Pyrenees, but how could they pass from any one of these regions to the others? The explanation is simple when we know that they are abundant within the Arctic circle, and when we consider further that our own country was once covered with ice as the polar lands are at the present time.

When the ice began to retreat northward the ground that was left exposed was soon invaded by an army of plants similar to those that clothe Arctic lands to-day. But as in the course of time the climate became gradually milder, more and more species advanced from the south, and the original plants which could endure cold but were not so well adapted to the new conditions, were pushed farther and farther north and higher and higher up the hillsides, till at last the only spots in the country where they could hold their own were the tops of the mountains in the vicinity of the snow line. There a few of them have lingered on to the present day, cut off from their kindred and with no possibility of colonising new ground. They link our own time with the ice age, and so form a fascinating chapter in the history of our land.

In the south-west corner of England, chiefly in Cornwall, but also to some extent in Devon and Dorset, and also in the west of Ireland, there is another isolated group of plants which have quite a different origin from these apline species. Their kith and kin live in Spain and Portugal, so as Portugal was formerly known as Lusitania, they have been named the Lusitanian flora. How, then, did they manage to cross the Bay of Biscay.

We know that in very ancient times England and Ireland were joined to Spain by a vast plain which stretched far to the west and is now covered by the ocean. It is believed, therefore, that these plants advanced northward from Lusitania across this low-lying land and that, when the ocean invaded it, those colonies only survived which had established themselves on the higher ground in the west of Ireland and in Cornwall. This may be true, but some of the plants, at any rate, are mountain lovers from the Pyrenees, and it is not likely that *they* would travel by such a route.

On the other hand, all of them have small seeds, so it is quite possible that they have been brought over in mud on the feet of migrating birds, and it is significant that none of the larger-seeded plants of Lusitania have been able to cross. So the problem of how the Lusitanian flora reached our islands is still a mystery, but perhaps you may one day be able to solve it.

The mere mention of some of the wild creatures I have brought together in this chapter is enough to fire the imagination of any young explorer. I hope it will inspire you with a desire to seek a more intimate acquaintance with them, and so provide you with an object for holiday trips into many parts of our country which otherwise you might not visit. But, unfortunately, in suggesting such adventures to you it is necessary for me to add a warning.

These species are rare. But they are rarer than they need be, because when a collector discovers one he thoughtlessly destroys it in order that he may bring home a specimen as a trophy. Every specimen so taken brings the species nearer to extinction, whereas if it had been left to complete its life naturally it would probably have produced many offspring. The true joy of nature-craft is not in the collection of skins or of dried plants, but in the knowing and understanding and loving of the living creature. So it should be a matter of honour among nature lovers, when they discover a rare thing, to rejoice in its existence and study it while they can, but to leave it in peace with the hope that it may prosper and multiply.

THE   END